A FAREWELL TO ARMS?

RUSSIA ▣ TRANSITION

A FAREWELL TO ARMS?

RUSSIA'S STRUGGLES WITH DEFENSE CONVERSION

BY **KEVIN P. O'PREY**

A TWENTIETH CENTURY FUND REPORT

1995 ◆ THE TWENTIETH CENTURY FUND PRESS ◆ NEW YORK

The Twentieth Century Fund sponsors and supervises timely analyses of economic policy, foreign affairs, and domestic political issues. Not-for-profit and nonpartisan, the Fund was founded in 1919 and endowed by Edward A. Filene.

Library of Congress Cataloging-in-Publication Data

O'Prey, Kevin P.
    A Farewell to arms: Russia's struggles with defense conversion
    / Kevin P. O'Prey.
        p. cm.--(Russia in Transition: 2)
    "A Twentieth Century Fund report."
    Includes index.
    ISBN 0-87078-375-0 (alk. paper)
    1. Economic conversion--Russia (Federation) 2. Defense
    industries--Russia (Federation) 3. Russia (Federation)--Economic
    policy--1991– 4. United States--Foreign economic relations--
    Russia (Federation) 5. Russia (Federation)--Foreign economic
    relations--United States. I. Title.
    HC340. 12z9d444   1995
    338.947--dc20   95–30961
                                                                   CIP

Cover Design: Claude Goodwin
Manufactured in the United States of America.

FOREWORD

The effort to reshape American foreign policy over the past six years has established at least one fact: that a world of new possibilities must inevitably be a world of uncertainties. The changes in international affairs set in motion by the transformation of the Soviet Union already have exceeded the expectations of even the most far-seeing observers of a decade ago. But, of course, we know only the beginning of the story. No longer an enigma wrapped in a riddle, the politics and economics of the Eurasian successors to the USSR remain more the object of conjecture than settled subjects.

The ultimate character of the key new state, the Russian Federation, is scarcely discernible at this stage. The events of the past few years have impressed upon us the complexity of the situation there. Three transformations are taking place simultaneously: the swift embrace of a dramatically more democratic form of government, the great leap from a command to a market economy, and the stunning withdrawal from a worldwide military standoff with the United States.

In view of the circumstances, the Trustees of the Twentieth Century Fund supported the notion of a special series, Russia in Transition, to examine selected topics from the extensive public policy agenda related to these changes. Our initial report, *Ecological Disaster: Cleaning Up the Hidden Legacy of the Soviet Regime* by Murray Feshbach, was published early in 1995. This monograph on defense conversion in Russia by Kevin O'Prey of MIT's Post-Soviet Security Project is the second of the series.

In the pages that follow, O'Prey defines conversion in the broadest sense as reallocation of human, physical, and financial resources to civilian pursuits. He makes clear that too often a more limited conception, say, of transforming factories or production lines, leads to faulty policymaking and practical frustration.

In Russia, O'Prey identifies three principal obstacles to rapid progress in defense conversion: technical difficulty of conversion, faulty government strategy and limited influence, and resistance of enterprise managers. He notes as well the special problems that exist because of the wrenching and fundamental nature of the changes going on in most aspects of Russian life. Moreover, unlike the winding down from cold war defense levels taking place in the United States, Russians must contend with both the much larger size of their defense sector, as a percentage of the total economy, and its considerably greater geographical concentration. Imagining the difficulties presented by the latter phenomenon, one need only think of the agonizing political struggles over base closings and defense plant reductions in America as not only multiplied in intensity but also taking place in a newly representative democracy. Even with our tested political system and thriving private economy, such events scarcely would be characterized by politicians taking the long view or citizens and businesses understanding the necessity to endure some economic pain for the greater good.

O'Prey also provides a useful and detailed road map of the industrial organization of the defense sector in Russia, including the structure of typical individual enterprises. He reviews the brief history of attempts to convert, starting with the command approach of the Gorbachev era. His account is likely to provide fresh insights into the daunting nature of the problem of conversion and the current weaknesses of the Russian state.

Though the way has been steep, there is substantial progress to report. Emphasizing the importance to American interests of successful conversion in Russia, O'Prey makes a realistic case for U.S. private industry and public agencies to offer larger contributions to the process. He believes that the West, especially the United States, can achieve much of value by ensuring that an institution already in existence, the Defense Enterprise Fund, is bolstered and enlarged.

Few would argue with O'Prey's overall contention that defense conversion is a key to market reform and thus to the establishment of a firm base for democratic capitalism in Russia. Despite the current political mood in Washington—one that seems to gainsay forceful American action in international affairs—O'Prey is surely on the right track. One can hope that his effort helps to rekindle a desire in American political circles to vigorously debate the nation's role in Russia's transformation. If it does nothing else, his work should make readers more realistic about the problems of conversion. The fair-minded will, as well, be more appreciative of the fact that, even if the results seem few and slow, the effort under way in Russia should be admired and must be supported.

Later this year, the Fund will publish two more reports in the Russia in Transition series: a study of efforts to modernize and improve the country's health care system by David Powell of Harvard University and an analysis of the challenges confronting labor in Russia by Linda Cook of Boston University.

Finally, on behalf of the Trustees of the Twentieth Century Fund, I want to thank Kevin O'Prey for sharing his knowledge and insights on this important topic.

RICHARD C. LEONE, *President*
The Twentieth Century Fund
September 1995

Contents

ACKNOWLEDGMENTS

I f I have learned nothing else during the course of this project, I have discovered that the author's name on the cover in no way does justice to all the people that contribute to a book's creation. I, at least, could not have produced this monograph without the help of a number of very generous colleagues and friends.

At the Twentieth Century Fund, I would like to thank Greg Anrig, Steven Greenfield, and Jason Renker for shepherding the project through its various phases. Greg Anrig, Brewster Denny, and Richard Leone provided valuable comments on the original drafts of the manuscript, while Steven Greenfield did an outstanding job editing the text into shape.

I was also very fortunate to benefit from the help of three extraordinary colleagues who provided invaluable commentary, data, and moral support throughout the course of the project: Peter Almquist, Clifford Gaddy, and Brian Taylor. Each has set the standard for me in terms of professional excellence, intellectual enthusiasm, and selfless commitment to colleagues.

This study is based on dissertation research that I conducted at MIT under the guidance of Stephen Meyer, Donald Blackmer, and Clifford Gaddy. In particular, as director of the Project on Post-Soviet Security, Stephen Meyer has taught me to think critically and conceptually in conducting analyses that have practical import. Much of my original research has been conducted with the generous support of the Office of Net Assessment, U.S. Department of Defense. During the drafting of the manuscript, I enjoyed the financial support and hospitality of the Foreign Policy Studies program of the Brookings Institution, first as a research fellow and then later as special guest. John Steinbruner, Charlotte Baldwin, Clifford Gaddy, and Janne Nolan went out of their way to help make my tenure at Brookings an enormously valuable experience, both professionally and personally.

I would also like to thank Gennadiy Kotchetkov and the staff of the Conversion Center at the Institute for USA and Canada Studies (ISKAN) for hosting me during my research in Russia. Anatoliy Gur'yev, the deputy mayor of Perm', was not only a terrific host to my research in the Urals, but he has consistently provided me with an example of the kind of energetic, forward-looking person who is helping to build the New Russia.

Finally, words cannot express the gratitude I owe to my wife, Maren. Her support, caring, and excitement know no bounds. She also has enormous patience to indulge someone so prone to cranky writer's blocks, and still give it all incredible meaning. I dedicate this monograph to her.

INTRODUCTION

The economic conversion of the once great Soviet defense industrial complex to new civilian tasks began not with a bang but with the stamp of a bureaucrat. In an effort to enlist the defense sector in improving the availability of goods to long-neglected Soviet consumers, the USSR Council of Ministers in March 1988 ordered that 220 plants involved in food and light industry be transferred to the control of the defense complex. The Council of Ministers subsequently expanded upon this humble foray into conversion, asking defense industry generally to do more to better the state of the Soviet economy. General Secretary Mikhail Gorbachev adopted the idea and unveiled it as a component of "new thinking" in Soviet foreign and security policy in his historic speech to the United Nations in December 1988. By reorienting the USSR's cold war–driven industry, Gorbachev and his reformers hoped to improve relations with the West while reinvigorating the failing economic system at home. The successor Russian government picked up where Gorbachev left off in attempting to free the struggling economy from the demands of its defense industrial base and to convert industries serving the military to more productive civilian uses.

It is hardly surprising that Moscow's reformers would look to their defense industries for assistance. Military might—not economic strength—had been the basis for the Soviet Union's claim to superpower status during the cold war. The contribution of the managers, designers, and workers in the defense industries was so highly valued by Soviet leaders that the command economy essentially was designed with them at its center. Central economic planners provided them with the finest human and material resources that the USSR had to offer. By the mid-1970s, the defense industrialists had surpassed even the uniformed military in economic and political clout.

Although for three decades the Soviet Union had enormous success in competing with the United States and the West in a race of armaments and technology, by the 1980s its political leadership had come to the realization that the cold war formula for military security was seriously undermining the country's competitive standing. It was not merely a question of the need to reduce defense spending; rather, the very structure of the economy was unsound and required thorough reorganization. Thus, the conversion of the wealth of the defense sector to productive uses in the civil economy became one of the corner7stones of the new reform era. The newly freed resources were thought to be essential for economic recovery and, by extension, the success of the larger process of market reform and democratization.

Nearly a decade later, much has changed in the world: the USSR is gone and Gorbachev ousted; Moscow's relationship with the West, although still tentative, is much improved; and Russia has undertaken sweeping political and economic reforms. Yet the initial hopes and promise of a Soviet/Russian "peace dividend" have only partly been realized. The level of government spending on building arms has been cut dramatically. Many of the best engineers and workers in the defense sector, have, in effect, converted themselves by fleeing to new jobs in the commercial economy. Some reform-oriented defense enterprise managers have transformed their state enterprises into private commercial firms and have successfully retooled their plants for civil production.

But in other ways, the defense industries have proved to be remarkably resistant to change. Despite an economic and security revolution, virtually no defense enterprises have gone out of business, and four out of five Soviet-era managers still hold their positions.[1] Although this in itself would not necessarily be cause for concern, when coupled with the dismal performance of defense enterprises and the demands they place on the Russian government, it becomes very problematic. By the narrowest definition, there are woefully few examples of defense plants successfully adopting new civil tasks sufficient to replace their former defense production. The large majority of defense enterprises have proved on the contrary to be financially insolvent, incapable of supporting themselves. Although the defense industries have lost much of their political clout, the managers of enterprises have succeeded in entrenching themselves and protecting their perquisites by taking advantage of new opportunities offered by the opening of the political and economic system.

In the process, these defense managers and their political allies have become a substantial obstacle to reform both in their individual enterprises and in the defense sector generally. Though these managers can no longer necessarily dictate terms to the government, their resistance to fundamental change poses a number of threats to the larger reform project in Russia. First, defense enterprises, being for the most part financially inviable on their own, act as a considerable drag on the Russian economy by demanding assistance from the state and by tying up resources that could be used more effectively elsewhere. This assistance may come as direct state budget allocations, subsidies or "soft" credits in the form of loans at extremely favorable rates, or privileges, such as protection from privatization or foreign competition. Direct financial assistance from the federal government places substantial strain on the already cash-strapped federal budget,[2] and implies taking away resources that could have been devoted to tasks such as providing a social safety net to cushion or retrain workers dislocated by Russia's transition.

Alternatively, credits and loans to enterprises from the Russian Central Bank expand the money supply and fuel inflation at a time when the government is attempting to maintain monetary restraint. Special privileges granted to defense enterprises are similarly problematic, albeit in more subtle ways. For example, restrictions on the privatization of defense enterprises prevent potentially viable businesses from spinning off from failing enterprises. Import protection measures such as tariffs impose a hidden burden on Russian consumers and nondefense businesses. And "off-budget financing"—the diversion of funds external to the formal state budget—fuels government corruption and represents a loss to potentially more needy but less vocal parts of the economy.[3] Finally, delay in declaring insolvent enterprises bankrupt prevents the transfer to the civil economy of whatever technological, capital, real estate, and human resources these defense enterprises continue to control.

The persistence of large defense industries also presents problems for Russia's foreign relations and for the world community generally. As long as this large network of defense enterprises and workers dependent on them continues to exist, there will be constant political pressure on the Russian government to support the production of arms, even if they are not militarily needed. Russian domestic politics notwithstanding, high rates of defense production inevitably will be viewed as a military threat in the United States and the West. Such a development could renew East-West tensions and undermine many of the substantial gains made in the international security realm in the past decade. At the very least, international lenders will be far less willing to support the Russian economy if their assistance indirectly promotes high rates of defense expenditure.

Another concern is arms proliferation. One of the biggest dangers in the near term is that Russia's large defense industrial constituency will continue to pressure the government to permit unrestricted export of weapons. Beyond the menace of excess and sophisticated arms diffusing across the globe, the weapons trade also threatens—given the plethora of political and ethnic disputes in the former Soviet Union—to fuel conflicts on Russia's borders.

Lastly, dislocation in the Russian defense sector may ultimately endanger the prospects for democratization in Russia. Although many workers have already left, several million continue to depend upon financially insolvent defense enterprises. Assuming that weapons production does not resume at cold war rates and that conversion efforts continue to have only limited success, many of these workers will find themselves unemployed in the very near future. Thanks to the peculiar structure and geography of the post-Soviet defense sector, the effects of these potential layoffs will be concentrated in a number of Russian cities that are highly dependent upon local defense enterprises for employment. If and when insolvent defense enterprises shut down, it could result in a serious socioeconomic crisis for these regions. Although this problem has so far remained hypothetical, the risk remains that worker anger could complicate relations between the federal government and defense industry regions and obstruct the success of democratization and economic reform efforts in the future.

Why have conversion efforts had such minimal success, and why still the immense size of the defense industrial base in Russia? There are three basic reasons:

1. *The technical difficulty of conversion, especially in the Russian context.* Always a demanding task, the problem of conversion is even more complex in Russia due to the organizational legacies of the Soviet system, the negative side effects of the transformation of the macroeconomy, and the exceedingly narrow approach that Russians have adopted toward conversion: Most Russians—and many outside observers—restrict their definition of conversion to the development of new civilian products by existing defense enterprises. The definition of conversion used in this paper, by

contrast, is more encompassing, including any transfer of assets—people, technologies, capital, etc.—from the defense sector to new uses in the civil economy. Ideally, as described below, the ownership and management of these assets would shift to private, market-oriented hands as well.

2. *The Russian government's faulty strategy and limited influence.* The approach to conversion by the Soviet and Russian governments has either been misguided—focusing on converting individual defense plants—or ineffectual. In particular, although it often has had the best intentions, the Federation government has consistently been reluctant, and to some extent unable, to subject the defense industries to the same tough conditions as the rest of the economy. As a consequence, the process of economic and political reform has actually empowered the existing corps of defense enterprise managers and made them more difficult to influence.

3. *The entrenchment and resistance of enterprise managers.* Much of the explanation for the failures of conversion and reform in the Soviet/Russian defense sector can be found at the enterprise level—that of the defense industrial facilities themselves. Over time, the attitudes and economic strategies of the directors or managers of these facilities have had an increasingly central role in determining the fate of reform efforts. Unfortunately, because of both their socialization in the Soviet system and the persistence of nonmarket incentives, many managers have found it preferable to take advantage of "old methods"—such as playing excessively on their inside connections and demanding support from the government—to maintain their positions and minimize market-oriented changes to their organizations. In the process, they have stifled many of the potentially promising developments and market adaptation under way in the defense sector.

What steps are necessary to carry out effective defense conversion in Russia? The ability of many defense enterprise managers to resist large-scale overhaul of the sector suggests that a fundamentally new approach to the problem is almost certainly necessary. Most important, the Russian government should recognize that the existing structure and large number of defense enterprises are untenable in the new economic and security environment. In order to carry out the necessary transformation, the

Russian government will likely need to continue to implement the "shock therapy" of macroeconomic stabilization. However, in contrast to its previous efforts, the government should also directly facilitate full-scale restructuring at the microeconomic level of defense enterprises, affecting not only their internal organization but also their relationships to other enterprises, to the market, and to the state.[4]

To start off, the Russian government would be wise to undertake a "bottom-up" review of its security needs and economic abilities. From this, the government should determine which defense industrial capabilities are essential for Russian national security, and which are cold war excesses. Defense enterprises falling into the latter category should be denied their current privileges in terms of state subsidies, restrictions on private ownership, exemptions from antimonopoly enforcement, etc. Ideally, any new policy initiatives should encourage downsizing through layoffs or spinoffs, privatization, reorganization, and refocusing enterprise activity to meet legitimate demand instead of being supply-driven. The resulting firms should be more responsive to market forces, adapting to customers' needs and competing with one another in terms of products and prices rather than connections to the government. Those enterprises that are not able, or refuse, to adapt by themselves should be declared bankrupt and sold off wholly or piecemeal to owners who can make better use of their assets. Stern measures of this sort will be essential to induce existing managers to reform, to encourage new firms that have a market-oriented management, or to break the hold of recalcitrant defense managers over their enterprises.

In all likelihood, the Russian government and defense industry will not be able to carry out this transformation on their own. For example, new Russian firms and planned ventures are starved for investment and lack basic knowledge of how to operate in a competitive market environment. If left to their own devices, many of these new firms would almost certainly fail in short order. The Russian government cannot and probably should not become involved in microeconomic management decisions or financing. Russian bureaucrats are all too accustomed to such an interventionary role and have demonstrated that they can create many more problems than they solve. Although Moscow can create the legal and institutional basis for the conversion and restructuring of the defense sector, it nonetheless lacks the capacity for evaluating credit needs rationally and is not set up to instill the entrepreneurialism, sound business judgment, and managerial skills and safeguards necessary for long-term success.

U.S. private industry and government, however, can make critical contributions in these areas. The transformation of Russian defense industry does not require a massive, Marshall Plan-type aid program, even if such an effort were politically feasible. Instead, the U.S. private sector, by forming joint ventures and industrial partnerships with new Russian firms, can provide much-needed investment as well as business knowledge to Russian industry. If the joint projects offer sufficient profit motive to the American partners, these partnerships should be able to sustain themselves over the long-term. And the joint venture mechanism should motivate current defense managers to restructure and convert their facilities to commercial work. Furthermore, the success of any joint ventures should have a profound signaling effect in the Russian defense sector, demonstrating to other managers and potential entrepreneurs that their future lies with the market, not the state. Similarly, Western businesses would discover through the example of working joint ventures that investment in Russia can be fruitful.

Although a number of U.S. firms have already developed such ventures, many more have held back in acknowledgment of the risks of investing in Russia. Here Washington can help greatly by providing these firms with seed capital. Instead of a large-scale aid program, the U.S. government would be making a small, initial investment to assist business partnerships in getting off the ground. In the longer term, there are a number of private mechanisms that could be developed to take responsibility for these tasks out of the government's hands. Thus, conversion assistance is one area where a relatively small amount of government investment can create the momentum necessary to encourage much larger commitments from the private sector.

THE U.S. INTEREST

At a time when the decline of the defense sector is a concern in the United States and traditional foreign aid programs are politically unpopular, inevitably there will be questions as to why the United States should be assisting defense industry conversion in Russia. In fact, the United States has a number of substantial interests in successful Russian restructuring and conversion, ranging from simple calculations of national security to the mutual interests of U.S. and Russian business to our broader stake in the success of Russian economic and political reforms.

In a number of fundamental ways, U.S. and Western security will be enhanced by the successful civilizing of the Russian defense industrial base. A large defense industrial capability provides a state with the potential to generate—or regenerate—a substantial military threat in a relatively short period. If this capability is dismantled, the amount of warning time to other states in case of a security threat is increased, and the higher economic costs of an arms buildup may cause a potential aggressor state to think twice about its ambitions.

In the near term, the persistence of a large defense industrial base in Russia—and other countries, for that matter—poses another, less obvious, threat to international security. Like the representatives of any other economic sector in decline, defense industrialists are an interest group that seeks support from the state. In contrast to garment workers, however, defense managers seek remedies that could, in calling for more weapons production, lead to an arms race, or at least hinder the easing of international tensions through arms reductions. Furthermore, as domestic demand declines, arms manufacturers naturally look abroad for markets. Unfortunately, in the process they contribute to proliferation of advanced technologies and armaments around the world, a process that helps stoke regional conflicts.

Most important, efforts to convert and restructure the Russian defense industrial base may play a key role in the success of market reform and, ultimately, democratization. The elimination of the various subsidies—hidden or otherwise—exemptions, and privileges provided by the state to the defense sector will permit the redistribution of these benefits to the general economy and society at large. Furthermore, the freeing up of economic and human resources currently held by industries serving the military should at the very least provide for increased mobility in the Russian capital, labor, and real estate markets. On the other side of the equation, if large numbers of defense workers do not succeed in finding new work—either in their former plants or in the larger economy—then, given the peculiar geography of Russian manufacturing, there is a real risk of unemployment-driven political instability in a number of Russian regions. To the extent that such instability interferes with the Russian government's efforts to foster a healthy market economy or produces popular support for reactionary political groups like Vladimir Zhirinovskiy's Liberal Democrats, the process of building up democracy in Russia will be all the more difficult.

On the positive side, cooperation in conversion offers potentially huge opportunities to both the U.S. and Russian business communities. The defense sector is the repository for much of the former Soviet Union's best research and technologies. Western high-technology firms can benefit by tapping into its strengths. Through conversion joint ventures Western businesses can also gain a foothold in Russia's immense domestic market, which offers 150 million consumers who long have been starved of consumer goods and services. Finally, the rebuilding of Russia's decrepit infrastructure supplies a task for conversion partnerships that could provide Western firms with an investment bonanza.

This study will consider the successes and failures of conversion in the Soviet Union and Russia, explanations for why the initial hopes and expectations for conversion have not been realized, and the measures that Russia and the United States can adopt to carry out conversion more effectively in the future.

CHAPTER 1

THE NATURE AND SCOPE OF THE CONVERSION PROBLEM IN RUSSIA

DEFINING CONVERSION

The definition that is assigned to conversion will have a critical bearing on the particular policies that a state will pursue, not to mention the likelihood of their success on the specified terms. Unfortunately, in Russia and elsewhere, discussions of conversion usually are based on a narrow and exceedingly optimistic definition of the concept. This common definition views conversion as a premeditated *reprofiling* or reuse of existing defense production or research facilities for civilian tasks. Reprofiling entails the reorienting or retooling of a plant's production lines and the retraining of its workers for civilian manufacturing.[1] For example, a tank plant might reorganize its production lines to produce tractors while a shipyard could switch from manufacturing destroyers to cargo vessels.

Yet historical experience in the United States, Western Europe, and Russia provides considerable evidence that successful defense plant reprofiling efforts in real life are very rare. It turns out that even the seemingly simple tanks/tractors or destroyers/cargo vessels shift is extremely difficult. More generally, reprofiling of existing facilities to make new products is a demanding undertaking for any manufacturing plant. Empirical evidence indicates that diversification to relatively similar manufactures within a plant producing for the commercial market on average is successful only half of the time.[2] Production establishments tend to be very specialized, possessing fixed capital and resources that cannot be easily shifted as a package to other activities. Thus, for example, when U.S. firms seek to diversify and enter new markets, they are much more likely to build a new plant rather than reprofile an existing one.[3]

The record for plant reprofiling in the defense sector is even worse. Attempts by defense plants to initiate manufacture of new products for civilian consumption have experienced a meager 20 percent success rate.[4] The reasons for this particularly low rate of success are related to the unique nature of defense work and its peculiar management biases and plant organization. Defense firms or enterprises typically differ from their civil counterparts because they have only a single customer—the government—that clearly specifies the types of products that it requires. Defense managers tend to have insufficient experience in assessing product demand when they foray into commercial markets. Because of the special defense-government relationship, the defense producer is also subject to intrusive government regulations and restrictions that do not exist in civil/commercial work.[5] Moreover, the actual process of designing new products is unique in defense work. The military customer and weapons designers often strive for the highest performance possible for the final product, with relatively less concern about its affordability.[6] Thus, defense conversion efforts often result in new products that are exceedingly expensive and have relatively little market appeal.

EXPANDING THE DEFINITION

Arguably, reprofiling is only one aspect of the much broader conversion phenomenon. Defense industrial conversion can be considered from three different hierarchical levels of analysis: the production establishment (plant), the firm or sector, and the macroeconomy. Reprofiling is conversion at the level of the production establishment. At the middle level is the restructuring of the defense sector by reorganizing existing firms to engage in new civilian business. At the macro level, conversion entails the shift of defense resources in the broadest terms to civil uses (see Figure 1.1)[7]. For each of these levels, it is perhaps most useful to define conversion in terms of outcomes—what works—rather than processes.

Given its practical limitations, the narrow—reprofiling—definition of conversion is not particularly helpful for resolving the problems of the defense industrial legacy of the cold war. Instead, it is more revealing to look to the other two levels of analysis—sectoral/firm restructuring and macroeconomic redistribution and adjustment—for the more promising opportunities. These levels of analysis provide a

---

FIGURE 1.1

LEVELS OF DEFENSE CONVERSION

♦ **MACROECONOMIC CONVERSION**
Redistribution of resources from defense to civil uses within
the macroeconomy—includes movement of labor, financial,
and material resources, etc.

♦ **SECTORAL AND FIRM RESTRUCTURING**
Reorganization of branches of industry and firms
for increased civilian output

♦ **PLANT REPROFILING**
Reorganization of specific production establishments,
institutes, and design facilities
for increased civilian output

Source: Derived from Robert M. Wallet, *Realizing the Peace Dividend:
A Systems Perspective on Defense Conversion.*

---

broader perspective on defense industrial conversion as a process of
utilizing as many of the sector's resources as possible for the development of the civil/commercial economy. Such resources include raw
materials, factory capacity, dual-use technologies—like composite
materials and electronics—and, most important, human capital:
world-class scientists and engineers, as well as educated workers. Not
all of these resources and capacities can be transferred to productive
uses. Some of them, in fact, may be liabilities.[8]

Unfortunately, one of the implications of this broader approach is
that it is not always possible to reprofile a particular defense plant nor
save the jobs of its workers. Defense firms may find that they are better off shutting down their plants and opening up brand-new operations elsewhere. Yet this is no different from the situation facing
declining nondefense industries. In the United States, moreover, the
process of mergers, acquisitions, and streamlining of defense industries in recent years has generated impressive results, yielding leaner,

more productive prime defense contractors. This success for the national economy has occurred despite the generally poor performance by U.S. defense firms in reprofiling.[9]

THE SOVIET LEGACY AND CONVERSION IN RUSSIA

Russia shares with the Western industrialized countries all the typical problems of defense conversion described above. However, the legacy of the Soviet Union has made the conversion task for Russia quantitatively and qualitatively even more difficult. The size of the Russian defense sector—and the number of people who depend on it for work or welfare—is enormous, making the task substantially more demanding than elsewhere.

Conversion in Russia is also more complex because it is occurring simultaneously with the fundamental transformation of the former Soviet Union's economy. The underdeveloped nature of Russia's new market mechanisms—capital markets, enterprising firms, contractual relationships, and so forth—has created an economic environment that often borders on chaos. Organized to operate according to the logic of the Soviet command economy, the vast majority of Russian defense enterprises are not fit to survive in market conditions. Finally, conversion requires a large financial commitment from Moscow, even if only to cushion the shock of worker dislocation. Yet the upheavals of reshaping the economy have left the Russian government essentially bankrupt.

THE SIZE OF THE SOVIET/RUSSIAN DEFENSE SECTOR

When the Soviet Union disintegrated, Russia inherited the lion's share of the industrial component of its defense establishment. Nearly 80 percent of the Soviet defense industries were located on Russian territory. Although Western economists and intelligence analysts could never agree on the precise size of the Soviet economy or defense sector during the cold war, there was complete harmony in the conclusion that the latter was much larger as a proportion of gross national product than anything in the West.[10] Politburo member Yegor Ligachev reported in May 1990 that the USSR had been spending 13–15 percent of its gross national product on defense.[11] Other, Western observers have argued that the actual proportion was something on the order of 20 percent of Soviet GNP or more.[12] In contrast, at the height of the Reagan arms buildup, the United States spent roughly 6 percent of

GNP on defense, and the other members of NATO were spending annually 3 percent of GNP on average during the mid-1980s.

The Soviet defense establishment's infrastructure by all accounts was enormous. The nine branches of the Soviet defense industries—the so-called *devyatka*—comprised between 2,000 and 4,000 production enterprises, research and development (R&D) facilities, and research institutes.[13] Estimates of the number of people who worked in these organizations during their heyday range from 9 million to 14 million.[14] By way of comparison, in 1990 defense industry work in the United States provided employment to only 1.5 to 1.9 million people.[15] The military-oriented industries dominated the Soviet manufacturing and high-technology sectors. Defense enterprises were responsible for 60 percent of all machine production and more than 80 percent of Soviet electronics production.[16] Although U.S. industry does not have a classification comparable to machine building, as an illustrative comparison, defense work accounts for only roughly 16 percent of work in the electronics component sector.[17]

These numbers, however, do not adequately convey the dysfunctional organizational and structural legacies of the Soviet system. Defense and heavy industry were the beneficiaries of an extremely unbalanced growth strategy that persisted in the USSR for more than fifty years.[18] The centralized, command nature of the Soviet economy was built upon a network of industrial bureaucracies and enterprises that have no use in a free market system. As a general principle, the industrial sectors and enterprises were organized to be efficiently commanded from the central bureaucracy and to achieve immense economies of scale. This mode of economic organization has created substantial impediments to the Russian defense establishment's performance in market competition.

THE PRIVILEGES OF THE SOVIET DEFENSE SECTOR

In an economic system designed to support priority sectors or causes, the defense industries were consistently top-drawer. Owing to the virtually unquestioning support of the Politburo leadership throughout the cold war period, the defense industries were provided with prime access to the finest material and human resources in the Soviet Union. Given the persistence of shortages and scarcity of resources in the economy, timely supply of raw and intermediate materials, as well as having first call on top managers and workers, was an invaluable benefit.[19] Although there may have been an element of coercion involved in recruiting, there were actually some substantial incentives to attract quality managers and workers. For one, defense work was very prestigious. Defense designers and engineers worked with the most advanced technologies in the USSR on tasks that the government heralded as vital for the security of the country and for socialism. Average salaries for managers and workers in industries supplying the military were similar to those in civil sectors, but defense work generally offered superior social benefits such as apartments, cars, consumer goods, access to vacation resorts, and so forth.[20]

The favoritism shown to the defense sector came at the price of underdevelopment in the rest of the Soviet economy. Because the defense industries would claim the highest-caliber engineers and best-quality raw materials, other sectors were left to make due with that which was residual.[21] As Gertrude Schroeder describes, the cost of a first world defense sector was a second world capital goods sector and a third world consumer sector with peculiarly socialist features.[22]

Ironically, the political clout of the defense industries during the 1970s and early 1980s was so powerful that their managers were often able to ignore the requests of their ultimate customer—the general staff of the military. After glasnost, numerous military officials stepped forward with tales of designers paying little attention to the weapons procurement orders and specifications provided by the armed forces. In a number of cases, they complained, the defense industrialists had convinced the political leadership to order weapons for which the military had no use or desire.[23] Industry's attitude was best summed up in a remark made by the chairman of the Military Industrial Commission, Igor Belousov, "The military has to be given not what they want, but what is necessary."[24]

ORGANIZATIONAL LEGACY

One of the most unfortunate remnants of the command economic system is the bizarre organization of Russian industry. In order to enhance the effectiveness of the command mechanisms at the center, the industrial sectors were divided into separate branches that fell under the direction of industrial ministries. Each sector or branch was organized hierarchically, with groups of enterprises receiving orders and supplies from their branch ministry. The management of the enterprise was responsible for meeting its assigned production targets, keeping its own books of financial accounts, and assuming various responsibilities regarding wages and bonuses, reinvestment of profits, and the like. Each of the nine branch ministries, in turn, was responsible for negotiating the planning targets for its industry, obtaining the material and financial resources required to fulfill these targets, inducing its enterprises to meet the plan, as well as organizing relationships between enterprises within the sector.[25] These branch ministries fell under the direction and oversight of the Military Industrial Commission (*Voyenno-Promyshlennaya Komissiya*—VPK) and the State Committee for Planning (*Gosplan*) (see Figure 1.2, below, and Figure 1.3, next page).

The branch ministerial organization was problematic in that it minimized horizontal integration across sectors, which is a common

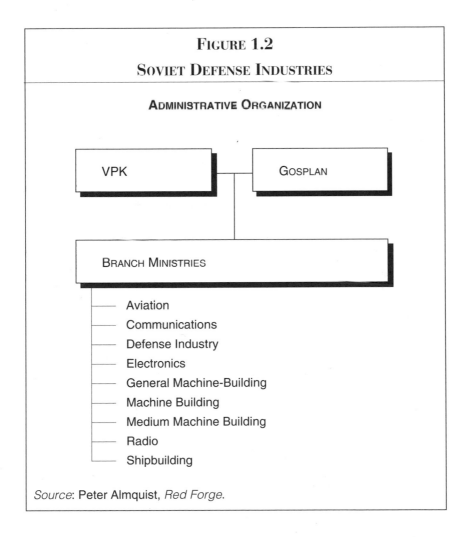

FIGURE 1.2

SOVIET DEFENSE INDUSTRIES

ADMINISTRATIVE ORGANIZATION

VPK

GOSPLAN

BRANCH MINISTRIES

—— Aviation

—— Communications

—— Defense Industry

—— Electronics

—— General Machine-Building

—— Machine Building

—— Medium Machine Building

—— Radio

—— Shipbuilding

Source: Peter Almquist, *Red Forge*.

feature in other industrialized economies. Plants located next door
to one another conceivably had absolutely no contact between them
if they were subordinated to different industrial ministries.[26] For
example, an aircraft plant would not communicate with a nearby
electronics manufacturer even if it were in need of microcircuits.
Instead, it would look to the aviation industry branch ministry for the
required supplies, even though the aviation-affiliated plant manufacturing them might be located on the other side of the country. The
relative costs of the products—including the real cost of transport—
were never a consideration.[27]

The unfortunate legacy of this system of organization is an unnatu-
ral series of monopolies in supply relationships that at times strangled
production in the Soviet system, and that constrain adjustment and

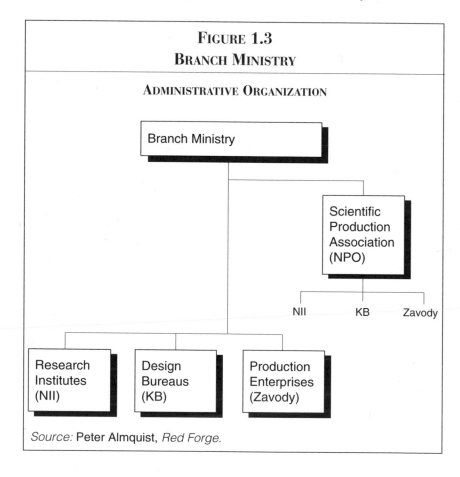

Figure 1.3
Branch Ministry

Administrative Organization

Branch Ministry

Scientific Production Association (NPO)

NII   KB   Zavody

Research Institutes (NII)

Design Bureaus (KB)

Production Enterprises (Zavody)

Source: **Peter Almquist,** *Red Forge.*

adaptation today. Although there were redundant production capacities across the various branches, because of minimal horizontal integration enterprises often relied upon a hierarchical chain of single suppliers, each of which had a monopoly on production *within its branch*. The practically nonexistent flow of information across the branches limited managers' and planners' awareness of existing resources and created a "false" scarcity in both the defense sector and the economy generally.[28] Even though the ministries were abolished at the end of the Soviet period, the pattern of minimal horizontal integration, information shortages, and artificial monopolies remains.[29] In the current environment, enterprise managers still rely inordinately upon informal networks within their former branches for supplies and for locating potential consumers.

THE STRUCTURE OF ENTERPRISES

Another profound legacy of the Soviet economy that complicates conversion is the inefficient structure of the enterprises themselves. Soviet-era enterprises—defense and civil—were by no means firms in the Western sense. Instead, as Gertrude Schroeder argues, they were agents of the state. In contrast to Western-type firms, which respond to market stimuli such as prices, Soviet enterprises did not face competition. Relationships between producers and their suppliers and customers were essentially bureaucratic in nature.[30]

The sometimes contradictory organizing principles of Soviet enterprises were specialization, concentration, and economies of scale. As a consequence, Soviet enterprises typically lacked various features that are essential for firms in a market economy. Because the branch ministry and state committees provided all of their planning functions, enterprise managements had very limited autonomy. With no forum for competition, they never developed market research capabilities for product development decisions, marketing departments to promote their wares, or a culture that emphasized affordability in product design.

Perhaps more problematic in the short run, because of the priority on specialization of facilities, individual enterprises were dependent on others for critical tasks. Research, design/development, and production facilities were generally organizationally distinct and not geographically related. (Figure 1.3 depicts the different types of enterprises in the Soviet economy.) For example, an Antonov transport aircraft might be the product of basic research conducted at an institute (*nauch-*

no-issledovatelskiy institut—NII) in Moscow, design and development at a design bureau (*konstruktorskoye byuro*—KB) in Kiev, Ukraine, and actual manufacture in a factory (*zavod*) in Ulyanovsk. As a result, today no one of these organizations can continue working productively without intensive cooperation from its traditional partners. Alternatively, they must replace their partners' contribution with either their own newly developed capacity or a new partner. A Russian enterprise today, therefore, resembles more a single production or design establishment within a larger firm rather than a fully integrated firm itself.[31]

The goals of concentration and economies of scale created enterprises of immense size. Within the defense industries there were approximately one hundred enterprises with more than ten thousand employees.[32] For example, the Krasnoye Sormovo Shipyard Production Association in Nizhniy Novgorod (formerly Gorkiy), a producer of submarines, in 1992 employed approximately thirty thousand workers. The Moscow Znamya Truda ("Banner of Labor") Machine Building Plant, a producer of MiG fighter aircraft, reportedly employed thirty thousand workers in 1990.[33] In contrast, it appears that there exists not one U.S. industrial establishment with more than ten thousand employees.[34]

The flip side of this industry concentration is the remarkable absence of small enterprises in Russian defense industry.[35] In a 1993 evaluation of 600 enterprises undergoing conversion, for example, less than 6 percent employed fewer than one thousand employees.[36] Such small and medium-sized enterprises are often described as the driving force for innovation in the U.S. economy and are well represented in the U.S. defense sector.[37]

Post-Soviet defense production enterprises tend to be organizationally bloated compared to typical Western firms. First, scarcity in the supply system created pressure for self-sufficiency in material inputs—autarky—within both enterprises and sectors. Enterprise managers and ministry bureaucrats reduced their risk that supply delays would interfere with their ability to meet planned production targets by internalizing as much of their sourcing as possible. Consequently, the benefits of division of labor and specialization were lost as enterprises developed redundant and often menial capabilities.[38] The Izhevsk Mechanical Plant is one example of such autarky. A producer of tactical missiles, the plant possesses shops for manufacturing all of the electronic components for the weapons as well as virtually all of the tools used in their fabrication.[39]

Second, Soviet defense enterprises provided social support services to their workers that are more typical of local governments and private transactions in the West. In the majority of cases, the defense worker and family would depend on the enterprise for housing, hospitals, kindergartens, and even vacation facilities. The Leninets Holding Company, for instance, provided its workers with an educational center, a hotel, and recreation centers "throughout the world." Like many other enterprises, Leninets also possessed a farm to produce food for its ministry, workers, even for the region as a whole.[40]

Because some of these functions are critical to the welfare of the local community, it has been vitally important during the transition not to let them collapse. Yet they are extremely expensive to maintain and add burdensome overhead to the core activities of defense enterprises. One defense industry official reports that 9 to 25 percent of funds budgeted to the defense complex by the central government are used for maintaining the social infrastructure.[41] A Russian economist observes that in some enterprises the social welfare component employs more than 20 percent of the plant's staff.[42]

THE REGIONAL DIMENSION

The Russian conversion problem is further complicated by its unique regional dimension. Although some defense industry analysts have highlighted the socioeconomic and political difficulties of the so-called industrial gun belt in the United States,[43] the nature of the problem in Russia is considerably more severe. Because of the priority of the defense industry in the former Soviet development strategy, perhaps as many as seventy towns and small cities were developed around a single defense enterprise.[44] When the demand for defense output dropped off, most of these areas found themselves with perhaps tens of thousands of qualified workers each—and their families—and little work. Ten of these cities were part of the nuclear weapons complex. Because of the secrecy of their work, these nuclear cities were built exclusively for the task and actually had walls or fences erected around them.[45] Their specialization and isolation places them in an especially difficult position for adapting to the postcold war world.

Beyond the closed nuclear cities, the defense industries provided a large proportion of employment for a number of cities and regions. In the extreme case, the republic of Udmurtiya, located in central Russia between Moscow and the Urals, depended upon defense work to occupy 57 percent of its industrial labor force. Six other oblasts (the Russian equivalent, more or less, of a state in the

United States) depended upon defense industries for more than 40 percent of their industrial employment (see Table 1.1). In dramatic
contrast, defense work in 1991 accounted for only 8.3 percent of nonfarm, private-sector employment in the most defense-dependent state
in the United States, Connecticut.[46]

The intensity of dependence upon defense industries for jobs in
these areas makes the defense drawdown particularly worrisome.
Since most defense workers rely on their place of employment for
social services, the collapse of the industry thrusts a huge social burden
onto the backs of local governments at the same time that their tax
base is collapsing. The danger of social and political unrest in these
regions—the dynamic that contributed to the collapse of Germany's
Weimar Republic—is taken seriously by the federation government.
Although anecdotal evidence suggests that many of the nonnuclear

TABLE 1.1

DEFENSE INDUSTRY SHARE OF TOTAL OBLAST' INDUSTRIAL* EMPLOYMENT		ABSOLUTE NUMBER OF DEFENSE INDUSTRY WORKERS**	
1. Udmurtiya	57%	1. Sverdlovsk	350
2. Kaluga	47%	2. St. Petersburg (city)	318
3. Mari-El	46%	3. Moscow (city)	300
4. Novosibirsk	45%	4. Nizhniy Novgorod	257
5. Omsk	43%	5. Moscow Oblast'	225
6. Magadan	41%	6. Perm'	213
7. Voronezh	40%	7. Samara	212
8. Novgorod	39%	8. Novosibirsk	172
9. Perm'	38%	9. Tatarstan	172
10. Vladimir	37%	10. Udmurtiya	168

Sources: Julian Cooper, The Soviet Defence Industry: Conversion and Economic
Reform (New York: Council on Foreign Relations Press, 1991); and Clifford
Gaddy, unpublished trip notes, Summer 1992.

* Industrial employment includes manufacturing and mining.

** In thousands, Oblasts, unless otherwise indicated.

defense-dependent cities are coping with the cutbacks and the collapse in production thus far, Russian officials and defense industry
supporters continue to warn of the long-term threat.[47]

THE DIVERSIFIED DEFENSE INDUSTRIES

One Soviet legacy that might have helped the defense industries was
their long history of manufacturing goods for nondefense uses. In fact,
before the onset of reforms in the 1980s, a common estimate was that
40 percent of the Soviet defense sector's output was directed toward
civilian uses. Even in 1990, such enterprises produced more than 25
percent of all nonfood consumer goods in the USSR. It accounted for
all or most of the production in a number of categories of consumer
goods: radios, televisions, VCRs, tape recorders, sewing machines,
cameras, and washing machines.[48] Defense enterprises also had a
considerable role in providing capital goods, equipment for the agricultural sector, and machinery for the food processing industries.
According to Julian Cooper, more than four hundred enterprises (out
of two to four thousand) in the defense complex were engaged exclusively in civilian production.[49]

Surprisingly, however, this diversified nature has not provided
the defense industries with many advantages in enterprise reprofiling. Although civilian production often occurred in the same plant as
defense work, the organizational barriers between the two realms
were extremely large. In fact, generally speaking, the civil and defense
realms were characterized by entirely distinct and separate technological processes.[50]

Moreover, the unbalanced investment strategy was just as prevalent in defense as it was in the general economy. Within the defense
sector, civil production clearly was valued only insofar as it supported
defense work; for example, reserves for wartime mobilization.[51] By
assessing the same rates of overhead to civil and defense production,
enterprise managers in effect were subsidizing their defense work.[52]
Russian economist Yevgeniy Kuznetsov argues that defense industry
manufacturing in the area of high-tech, dual-use output—such as semiconductors and microelectronics—is generally of very low quality and
uncompetitive even in the internal Russian market, to say nothing of
foreign markets. Products in this category are highly dependent upon
military technology. There is, for instance, no civilian semiconductor
base in Russia per se, as the semiconductors that go to consumer goods

are merely those rejected for poor quality by defense industry consumers. Even the electronics that meet military specifications are generally considered to be inferior to technologies that are widely available
commercially in the West. As a consequence, Russian industrial customers generally can purchase cheaper, better-quality microcircuitry
abroad.[53]

According to Kuznetsov, there are some areas where defense
industry civilian production can be expanded successfully. One of
these may be heavy consumer durables. For production of automo-
biles, refrigerators, and the like, the civil manufacturing facility usually was constructed independently of the defense plant. The equipment
for this facility often was purchased almost entirely abroad—commonly East Germany—and, as a consequence, was more technologically advanced. The efficiency of the civil facility, however, was
hindered because its accounts were still routinely assessed high overhead charges to support the defense plant.[54] If the relationship
between the military and civilian plants were severed, it is conceiv-
able that the latter could successfully expand their production. Aircraft
and ships seem to be areas where expanded civil production from a
technical standpoint could be facilitated relatively easily.[55]

MARKET-ORIENTED ADJUSTMENT

On first glance, it appears difficult to determine whether excessive
militarization of the economy or its heritage of central planning puts
Russia at a greater disadvantage in undertaking conversion. But, as
the next chapter will describe, the history of Soviet and Russian
conversion efforts suggests that it has been the organizational contradictions of the command economy that have stifled the wide-scale
adjustment of defense enterprises to producing commercial goods in
a market economy. Perhaps a large part of the problem has been
Russia's focus on reprofiling, rather than sectoral/firm adjustment
and macroeconomic redistribution. This mistaken focus is to some
extent understandable because market-type firms did not exist in the
Soviet system. Since enterprises were the dominant type of organization, it stood to reason that they be the objects of conversion.

But if conversion is to succeed in the Russian context, this perspective must be expanded considerably. Arguably, command-sys-
tem-era enterprises are themselves part of the problem. Instead of
attempting to reprofile these usually poorly organized and inefficient

behemoths, Russia should be striving to restructure their components, creating new market-type firms. These new firms can take advantage of the valuable parts of the old enterprises without having to support the vestiges of the command system. This sort of market-oriented adjustment and adaptation is perhaps the only means by which the existing assets and personnel of the defense industries can cease being a burden on the Russian economy and start becoming an engine.

Chapter 2

The History of Conversion in the Soviet Union and Russia

Since 1987, the Soviet and then Russian political leaderships have engaged in considerable efforts to convert their defense industries to more productive civilian uses. These efforts have ranged from tinkering with the state economic plan during the Gorbachev period to dismantling the command system and cutting off the defense sector of much of its funding during the Gaydar "shock therapy" phase to a more mixed macroeconomic and structural reform approach that has been attempted since. The results of these policies have been somewhat positive in terms of economywide conversion. Yet success in restructuring at the sectoral and firm level has been limited, and at the level of enterprise reprofiling the record has been poor. Unfortunately the meager progress at the more localized levels threatens to undermine those gains that have been made on the broader scale.

The Command Approach: The Gorbachev Era

The first attempt to convert the Soviet economy was characterized by modest reform within the existing command system. Although General Secretary Mikhail Gorbachev and his government repeatedly flirted with the notion of radical market reform, they never quite embraced it. Rather, they sought to adjust the priorities of the existing system to perform better in more demanding, modern conditions. Although perestroika translates into English as restructuring, the Gorbachev reform process never took on the task of replacing the command system's ministries, state committees, and state enterprises with a market economy and

27

its related institutions. The fundamental assumptions of the command system were never sufficiently questioned. This reluctance ultimately spelled doom for the Gorbachev economic reform and defense conversion programs.[1]

An irony of the modest perestroika process was that Gorbachev had to dismantle many of the Communist party's instruments of control over society and the economy in order to carry out reform. Because this occurred simultaneously with the regime's alienating entrenched vested interests like state enterprise managers, the Gorbachev-era reformers were in a sense picking a fight that they could not win. In the end, the centrifugal forces of political and economic change sent the Soviet system spinning out of control. Defense enterprises only marginally benefited from their newfound autonomy, however, as the disorder in the system wreaked havoc upon their once privileged life as much as it freed them from rigid dictates from the Kremlin.

Conversion efforts in the Soviet Union began in earnest in 1987. At that time, the defense sector was widely perceived to be the one part of the economy that was working well. As a result, it became the model that policymakers applied to the underdeveloped civil sectors of the economy. In a variety of policy initiatives and Soviet-style campaigns they sought to transfer the magic of the defense industries to other sectors in order to jump-start the sputtering economy. The defense managers had proved themselves in competition with the West; thus, the logic went, by turning their attention to conversion products, the civil economy would be saved.

Throughout the Gorbachev period, the conversion program was a top-down reform initiated by the political leadership and carried out through traditional Soviet planning mechanisms. Under Prime Minister Nikolay Ryzhkov, early conversion efforts included the transfer of leading administrative personnel from the defense industry to prominent government posts that were responsible for important areas of the civil economy.[2] By October 1987, the Central Committee of the Communist Party, seeking to enhance the performance of the food processing sector, adopted a decision to transfer the 220 enterprises of the Ministry of Light and Food Industry to the responsibility of the defense industrial ministries.[3] Subsequently, the political leadership ordered the Military Industrial Commission (VPK) and State Planning Committee (Gosplan) to formulate a much larger, more comprehensive conversion program. Gorbachev later explained the logic behind the effort as one of catching up economically with the West:

for [the Soviet Union] to go to cheek-to-jowl with [the Americans], they [the Americans] would have to lie prostrate. All funds, materials, 75 percent of our best scientific efforts have been in the defense industry. This is a distorted, militarized economy. During the same time [the cold war], defeated Germany, Japan, Italy were developing their economies, converting their industries. That is why we must now make use of our productive and intellectual potential—let it be known how those in the defense industry worked.[4]

The essence of the comprehensive program was the further diversification of the defense sector by assigning greater civilian production responsibilities to the defense industrial ministries. The central planners in Gosplan set a goal of shifting the mix of production by the defense branches from 60 percent defense/40 percent civil in 1988 to 40 percent defense/60 percent civil in 1995.[5]

This top-down conversion approach produced decisions that were typical of the Soviet system, and were somewhat incomprehensible to outside observers. Bureaucrats in Moscow often selected new production tasks for enterprises irrespective of any obvious economic or technological logic, or common sense. In many cases, defense enterprises were assigned conversion tasks that had nothing to do with their engineering experience or plant capacities. For example, a Kiev facility that developed and produced Antonov transport aircraft found its aircraft orders suddenly terminated, only to be replaced by orders for machinery for packaging meat dumplings and bags of flour, equipment for freezing potatoes, animal pelt drying apparatus, and devices for cleaning root crops.[6] A jet engine design bureau was charged with developing and improving machines for the leather and fur industries.[7] Another defense design bureau was ordered to produce cabbage-seeding combines and to devise equipment to package dried fruit.[8] In 1989 the Central Committee secretary for defense industry matters (and 1991 coup plotter), Oleg Baklanov, decried such decisions when he complained that he had witnessed the "awful spectacle" of aviation engineers "practically on their knees" manufacturing baby strollers.[9]

The second thrust of reform that had an important impact on the defense industries during this period was the general efforts at restructuring (perestroika) of the entire Soviet economy. Although economic reform took many forms during Gorbachev's tenure, the most important measure with respect to the defense sector was the 1987 Law on the State

Enterprise. Taking effect on January 1, 1988, this law represented an effort to improve the management and economic efficiency of enterprises by permitting them greater autonomy from the ministries while demanding from them a greater degree of financial accountability. The law required that enterprises operate according to the principles of self-management and self-financing (*khozraschyot*), wherein they were responsible themselves for ensuring that their revenues covered their outlays. Enterprises that could not meet these requirements would be declared bankrupt and liquidated. In order to introduce greater workplace democracy, the law also required that the manager of the enterprise be elected by the worker collective.[10]

One of the main aims of the law was to cope with the problem of "soft-budget constraints" in enterprises. As first explained by Janos Kornai, enterprises in Soviet-type economies tend to ignore market signals and consistently operate at an economic loss. Enterprise managers generally do not have to obtain revenues sufficient to cover their operating costs because they are confident of the reliability of external (that is, state) assistance, thus absolving them of responsibility for profitable operation.[11] By reducing state interventions and attempting to increase their direct responsibility over the affairs of the enterprise, the Law on the State Enterprise aimed to create more businesslike, "hard-budget" constraints on managers.

Furthermore, the 1988 Law on Cooperatives permitted enterprises to organize "cooperatives": organizations attached to the enterprise that could engage in quasi-independent activity. Often operating under a lease agreement with their founding enterprise or ministry, cooperatives were not subject to compulsory plan assignments and had substantial freedom to set their own wages and prices, all the while having access to the centralized supply system.[12]

Both aspects of reform during the Gorbachev period failed and, in some respects, made the situation worse for everyone. The Gorbachev strategy for conversion turned out to be an unmitigated disaster. Not only were there very few cases of a successful new commercial product being developed at a defense plant, but the campaign had the effect of overstressing the defense industrial planning system and in many cases interfering with the ability of managers to carry out their defense work. Because of the combined effects of conversion difficulties and the larger collapse of command economic mechanisms, by 1991 the volume of civilian output in defense-sector enterprises—despite substantial resource allocations—was actually *dropping*.[13]

The Gorbachev conversion program appears also to have failed at the macroeconomic level. One of the ironies of the Gorbachev strategy is that budgetary and resource allocations to the defense industrial ministries may not have been reduced despite "conversion." It is clear that Gorbachev initiated a steep reduction in the level of weapons procurement in 1989.[14] But the increased allocations for new civil production by the defense industrial ministries may have completely made up for the decrease in military hardware. New civilian production proved costly as enterprise managers usually had to adopt or even develop for themselves new processes and technologies. Civilian production costs were driven up further because the defense industrial ministries and enterprises were not permitted to transfer their now idle defense assets to new civil tasks. The government ordered that defense production lines were vital reserve capacity in case of mobilization that could not be converted.[15]

Reprofiling efforts by defense enterprises were a miserable failure. There were widespread delays in getting new civil production up and running.[16] Part of the problem was that defense managers, operating without any knowledge of market demand or any history of developing projects with the customer in mind, simply had no idea what to do. When the reform-oriented St. Petersburg government sought to help local defense industry organize a regional conversion program in 1991, the effort foundered because the directors did not offer any proposals.[17]

When the managers actually undertook to convert their plants, the results were usually extremely expensive and poorly designed products for which there was little, if any, market demand. If they absolutely had to work on civil projects, many defense managers chose to develop new products so they could circumvent state price controls and pass their inflated costs on to consumers.[18] In a widely ridiculed case, a plant entrusted with manufacturing sausage-producing machines turned out a product that created green sausages. Another design bureau assigned to design washing machines developed a practically gold-plated model that had more than twenty cycles and cost three times more than the existing competition.[19] And finally, the director of the Sevmash submarine design and production complex in Severodvinsk offered a metaphor for the Soviet reprofiling experience when he came up with a civil product that was compatible with his military experience: he developed a tourist minisubmarine with windows.[20]

Although President Gorbachev, other senior political leaders, and outside analysts heaped considerable scorn on bureaucrats and defense enterprise managers for blocking conversion, the program appears to have been doomed from the start. Its fundamental flaw was the assumption that the command economic formula that produced success in the defense industries could somehow be applied to the civil economy. This ignored the fact that while the Soviet defense industries may have been effective at turning out competitive armaments, they were always very economically inefficient in doing so.[21] The defense sector achieved success because of the high priority that the Soviet political leadership and economic planning organs placed on them, at the cost of retarding the civil sector's development. When the time came to convert, the Soviet leadership sought to maintain the primacy of the defense sector *and* place fresh priority on the civil sector. Although this might be possible in a rapidly expanding economy, the Soviet economy in the late 1980s was shrinking.[22]

The other reason for the failure of the conversion program was its traditional, Soviet campaign-style approach. Although this method had had some success in the past, by 1989 central commands were increasingly disregarded by defense enterprises as well as republic, regional, and local governments.[23] Furthermore, the top-down approach was prone to technologically foolish decisions. In those places where orders were obeyed, the outcome was often unsuccessful.

Legal reforms affecting enterprises and the larger economy did not work entirely as expected. One of the main aims of efforts to improve the financial responsibility and performance of enterprises was increased autonomy for enterprise directors from ministerial meddling or oversight. Having been elected by their enterprises, defense managers could now lay claim to a legitimacy generated from outside ministerial channels. Managers also became inclined to devote their energies to their potentially more profitable cooperatives rather than to annoying state orders. Ultimately, the war of laws between the republic governments and Moscow and the collapse of the centralized supply system provided managers with the cover to disregard state orders or to inflate their prices, even for defense output.[24]

Yet in gaining their new autonomy, enterprise managers were not saddled with new responsibilities. Hard-budget constraints were never successfully imposed on the enterprises, and the threat of bankruptcy was not taken seriously. Resource prices, to take one example, continued to be fixed by the state, thereby indirectly subsidizing the enterprises.[25] Furthermore, the government continued to support the enterprises as before through state orders (accounting for as much as 90 percent of industrial output),[26] only now the enterprise managers increasingly could ignore the demands of the state. With this new autonomy, enterprise managers in defense and civilian industries did not prove themselves to be any more economy-minded than before.

As a consequence of this reform, the political leadership had sacrificed some of the levers it possessed over enterprises without gaining any improved economic performance. As enterprises increasingly ignored state orders, the stability and coherence of the command economy began to deteriorate. By 1991, the Soviet economy had become in a number of ways unresponsive to Moscow. Perestroika reform efforts proved to be half-measures at a time when radical steps were required.

YELTSIN AND GAYDAR: THE SHOCK AND REVIVE APPROACH

The disintegration of the Soviet Union in the wake of the failed August 1991 putsch permitted the Russian Federation to take economic reform matters into its own hands. Under the direction of President Boris Yeltsin and his chief economic reform strategist, Yegor Gaydar,[27] the Russian government set out on a course of fundamental reform that the Gorbachev regime had so assiduously avoided. The Gaydar strategy aimed to introduce market forces rapidly to the Russian economy by eliminating most of the command system's planning organs, liberalizing prices, privatizing state (including defense) enterprises, and pursuing macroeconomic stabilization through restrictive budgetary and monetary policy.

One of the central tenets of the Yeltsin-Gaydar reform was the removal of the state bureaucracy from day-to-day economic matters. The reformers effectively liberated most enterprises from constant interference by eliminating or downgrading the state industrial ministries.[28] Although other central planning organs persisted under new names, they clearly were stripped of much of their former authority. For example, although Gosplan became the Ministry of the Economy, the renamed body no longer wielded anything near its former influence on enterprise management.

The means by which Gaydar's "shock therapy" would induce changes in enterprise behavior and facilitate conversion differed fundamentally from that of the Gorbachev period. Abandoning the top-down, campaign approach, starting in January 1992, the government sought to limit its efforts initially to price liberalization and macroeconomic stabilization. By freeing prices and cutting off most state support, the logic went, enterprises would be exposed to hard-budget constraints and, as a result, would reorganize themselves and their work in order to operate efficiently in market conditions.

In the defense sector, as elsewhere, the government removed itself from directing or supporting enterprises. With the aim of forcing most defense enterprises to find new work in the civil sector or liquidate, the government slashed state orders for arms procurement by 68 percent.[29] The Russian government also adopted a new approach to conversion assistance by placing the primary creative and financial burden on the enterprises themselves.[30] During early 1992 the government offered an amount of official credits for conversion that was minuscule by the standards of Soviet-era subsidy. Moreover, the government awarded these credits only to specific proposals that it deemed to be worthy, rather than granting more general support to the defense industries.

Unfortunately, the "shock" phase of the Yeltsin-Gaydar reforms provoked the bitter opposition of the Russian Congress of Peoples Deputies, vested interests such as the enterprise managers and government bureaucrats, and most of the Gorbachev-era economic reformers. Yeltsin and Gaydar felt compelled to abandon strict macroeconomic stabilization policies by April-May 1992. The opposition was able to undermine the reforms by both economic and political means.

Perhaps the most devastating blow to radical reform came from the entrenched industrialists exerting economic pressure. Contrary to expectations, state-owned enterprises in the defense and civil sectors were able to frustrate the reform program in a matter of months. Although the government succeeded in liberalizing prices and pursuing a restrictive monetary policy during the first two months of 1992, state enterprises did not respond by restructuring. Instead, they took advantage of the liberalization by jacking up the prices for their output and increasing worker wages. Although enterprises now lacked the financial resources to pay one another for supplies and products, they honored each others' promissory notes and continued as before. By creating huge mutual debts, the enterprises were able to replace the government and Central Bank as the sources of credit emission. As a consequence, the government could not control the money supply, and inflation increased at the same time that production was squeezed. By April 1992, confronted with the prospect of wide-scale enterprise insolvency and under pressure from the Congress of People's Deputies, the government began once again to hand out huge subsidies to inefficient producers.[31]

Politically, the Congress of People's Deputies and the industrial lobby critics convinced Yeltsin before long to add industrialists to his government of reformers. After sacrificing First Deputy Prime Minister Gennadiy Burbulis in April, in June Yeltsin appointed two managers of defense enterprises and an energy sector bureaucrat—Georgiy Khizha, Vladimir Shumeyko, and Viktor Chernomyrdin—to the government.[32] Yeltsin also permitted a number of opponents of reform and supporters of industry to hold strategic government positions.[33] By exercising their newfound leverage and control as well as having Yeltsin's ear, these conservatives helped keep the government on a track of more gradual reform throughout the second half of 1992.

The final blow to radical reform came with the appointment of Viktor Gerashchenko to the post of head of the Russian Central Bank. The notion of macroeconomic stabilization became chimerical as, beginning in July 1992, Gerashchenko periodically released soft credits—usually loans at negative real interest rates—to all Russian industry. Gerashchenko's motivation was partly to help industrialists pay off their interenterprise debts, and partly to provide cash-strapped manufacturers with working capital.[34]

Despite the abandonment of the policies of shock therapy, Gaydar was nonetheless vilified in the legislature throughout 1992. In the approach to the December 1992 meeting of the Congress of People's Deputies, Gaydar sought a compromise with the lobby of industrialists, the Civic Union. Although the two sides reached an agreement in which the Civic Union would support Gaydar's assuming the role of prime minister, the accord collapsed before the Congress opened. Faced with widespread opposition, Yeltsin was forced to sacrifice Gaydar.

Political and economic difficulties confronting reformers during this period underlined just how monumental the task of transforming the old system would be. During 1992 Russian industrial production plummeted by 19 percent, while inflation soared to about 30 percent per month by the end of the year. Average real wages fell by around one-third compared to 1991, placing 35 percent of all Russians below the poverty line. The state budget deficit was approximately 10–15 percent of GDP.[35]

In terms of defense conversion, although the record was mixed, that was an improvement over the Gorbachev period. In particular, Yeltsin and Gaydar made substantial progress at the macro level by slashing state spending on weapons procurement. Although some of the gains made on this front were eroded by the subsequent release of credits to defense enterprises, the government at least had signaled to producers that the days of lavish spending on defense were over.

Success at the level of sectoral and firm restructuring was less evident. The reformers succeeded in abolishing many of the state planning organizations that had long interfered in day-to-day management decisions of enterprises. Beyond this, the government eschewed a direct assault on the defense industries.[36] Gaydar's strategy of letting tight fiscal and monetary conditions force adjustment on the sectors and enterprises did not take into account the debt-based trading between enterprises or the government's inability to hew to a restrictive monetary policy. Although enterprises came more to resemble employment centers rather than producers, by and large they minimized adjustment and muddled on.

Reprofiling efforts by defense enterprises generally fared as miserably as they had under Gorbachev. Although many defense managers by this time had realized that they would have to convert at least some of their facilities, they continued to show themselves as lacking insight into market demand. They also had to contend with the collapse of many of their supply relationships and orders, inflation, and worker flight. None of this made reprofiling any easier.

CHERNOMYRDIN'S "NO SHOCK, SOME THERAPY"

The replacement of Gaydar as prime minister by the energy industry's Viktor Chernomyrdin in December 1992 initially seemed to portend a retreat to old Soviet methods in industrial practice. However, Chernomyrdin's tenure has produced significant, if gradual, progress along the lines originally established by Gaydar. More importantly, during this period the government expanded upon Gaydar's program to impose microeconomic reforms upon defense enterprises. By the end of 1994, Russia had developed many aspects of a market economy, even if its performance was weak. Conversion results improved somewhat, if only because more time had passed, but still fell short of their potential.

Despite a minimum of genuine reformers in high positions, Chernomyrdin and his government maintained continuity with previous policies. Although weapons procurement cuts appeared to have tapered off, the new government demonstrated that it would not permit any increases in the defense budget. During the drawing up of the 1994 state budget, Chernomyrdin resisted strong political pressure from the Ministry of Defense and the defense industries to double the level of defense expenditures.[37] The official conversion program continued to put the onus on enterprises to find new products to support themselves. The state continued to offer some financial assistance for conversion programs that it approved, but only small amounts.

The government's record of macroeconomic stabilization was more checkered. Anders Åslund describes three phases with respect to the politics of macroeconomic stabilization: stalemate from June through September 1993 as the Ministry of Finance squared off with the free-spending parliament and Central Bank; a breakthrough for reformers from September 1993 to December 1993; and then slow decline during 1994 until the government again opted for stabilization after the collapse of the ruble on "Black Tuesday," October 11.[38] While Boris Fyodorov held the post of minister of finance (December 1992-January 1994), he aggressively sought to stem the amount of state assistance to defense and civil enterprises. He almost single-handedly kept the budget deficit under control by refusing to pay out new expenditures that were constantly being approved by government officials with no authority to do so.[39] Critics charged that Fyodorov also withheld legitimate expenditures until the end of the budgetary cycle in order to permit inflation to reduce the state's outlays.[40] In September 1993, Fyodorov officially banned all subsidized credits with a government decree.[41] President Yeltsin dispensed with the problem of a free-spending parliament when he first disbanded, then bombarded the Supreme Soviet in September– October 1993.

Fyodorov and other reformers had less success in curbing the Central Bank under Viktor Gerashchenko, who continued to think that Russia's problems would be solved if industry just received more aid. Fyodorov ultimately found it impossible to abolish subsidized credits, especially while Chernomyrdin backed Gerashchenko. Although the Central Bank finally was persuaded to charge a positive real interest rate on its credits in November 1993, thus bringing some measure of economic rationality into play, the decisive defeat of reform parties in the December 1993 parliamentary elections undermined their arguments. Fyodorov and Gaydar (recently rehabilitated politically, he had returned to the inner circle as minister of the economy in September 1993) resigned from the government in January 1994. Chernomyrdin was willing to maintain Fyodorov's budget policies thereafter, but he continued to grant Gerashchenko and the Central Bank considerable leeway for the provision of credits to industry. Chernomyrdin and his government appeared content with an annual inflation rate in the vicinity of 100 percent,[42] at least until it provoked a major currency crisis (Black Tuesday).

Defense Enterprise Privatization

The key aspect of Chernomyrdin's reforms that had been lacking during the Gaydar period was the direct pursuit of enterprise-level restructuring through privatization, beginning in February 1993. Reformers in the government believed that private ownership would finally establish hard-budget constraints over defense enterprises.[43] President Yeltsin asked Deputy Prime Minister Anatoliy Chubays, head of the State Committee for the Management of State Property (GKI), to privatize defense plants with a minimum of restrictions. Although the government added further restrictions to the program during the summer of 1993,[44] most defense enterprises were ordered to begin the process of privatization. By March 1994, approximately seven hundred enterprises had done so.

Table 2.1

Planned Ownership Status of Russian Defense Enterprises at the End of 1994

State-owned enterprises exempt from privatization	450
"Corporatized" plants in which the state will hold the majority share for 3 years (Corporatized I)	150
"Corporatized" plants in which the state will possess veto authority over managerial decisions (Corporatized II)	600
"Private" enterprises[*]	800
Total number of defense enterprises (All numbers are approximate)	2,000

Source: Alfred Koch, deputy chairman of the GKI, as cited in Keith Bush, "Most Defense Enterprises to Be Privatized by End 1994," Radio Free Europe/Radio Liberty Daily Report, March 1, 1994.

[*] Includes 700 enterprises privatized as of March 1, 1994 and approximately 100 enterprises scheduled to be privatized by January 1995.

According to the government's plan, by the end of 1994 more than three-quarters of all defense enterprises were to have begun privatizing.[45]

TYPES OF OWNERSHIP

There are essentially three types of ownership status for defense enterprises today: state-owned, "corporatized," and private. Table 2.1 and Figure 2.1 present an approximate breakdown of the number of enterprises in each category.

State-owned Enterprises. According to an August 1993 presidential decree governing defense industry privatization, 482 enterprises were forbidden to privatize. These enterprises will continue to be the

FIGURE 2.1

PLANNED OWNERSHIP STATUS OF RUSSIAN DEFENSE ENTERPRISES AT THE END OF 1994

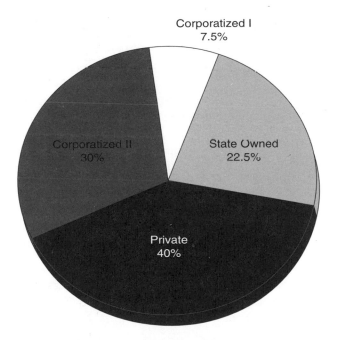

Source: Alfred Koch, as cited in Keith Bush, "Most Defense Enterprises to Be Privatized by End 1994."

property of the Russian government. The State Committee on Defense Branches of Industry (Goskomoboronprom) directly oversees their management on the behalf of the GKI.[46]

By law all those defense enterprises not on the list have been required to initiate the process of privatization. In the vast majority of cases this entailed a decision by the management and worker collective to privatize according to the so-called second option, in which 51 percent of shares are made available to the enterprise's staff (workers and management).[47] The remaining shares would be auctioned off or retained by the state.

"Corporatized" Enterprises. Corporatized enterprises are those that have begun the process of privatization—becoming joint-stock companies (*aktsionernyye obshchestva*—AOs)—but are not yet fully private. In the first category of corporatized enterprises (Corporatized I), 150 enterprises have become joint-stock companies in which the state holds the absolute majority of ownership shares.

In the second category (Corporatized II), there are about six hundred enterprises in which the state will hold a "golden share" of stock through at least the fall of 1996. This "golden share" would be no more than 20 percent of the enterprise's stock, but it represents a state veto authority over the affairs of the enterprise. Goskomoboronprom would again be the state's agent. However, assuming that the general director is not contradicting the larger goals of the Russian government—and Goskomoboronprom, in particular—the state commonly appears to transfer the de facto control of its packet to the enterprise management.[48]

Private Enterprises. The last category of enterprises contains those that are fully private. The state does not legally possess any authority over the decisions of management. However, if the enterprise is producing for military purposes, its manager must be certified by Goskomoboronprom. This is essentially a licensing arrangement that protects the state's interests in fully private defense enterprises.[49]

EVALUATING THE EFFORT TO SHRINK AND RESTRUCTURE THE DEFENSE SECTOR

MACROECONOMIC CONVERSION

According to a number of macroeconomic indicators, an impressive amount of defense conversion has occurred in the Russian economy. According to official Russian estimates, the share of military-related production in the total output of Russian defense industries will have been only 17–18 percent in 1994, having dropped from 68 percent in 1989 (see Table 2.2 and Figure 2.2).

TABLE 2.2

PERCENTAGE OF DEFENSE ENTERPRISE OUTPUT PRODUCED FOR STATE DEFENSE ORDERS

Share of Output for Defense Orders (in comparable prices)

1989	1990	1991	1992	1993 (expected)	1994 (forecast)
68.4	49.7	38.3	25.8	20.7	17–18.5

For all Defense Branches of Industry of the Russian Federation

Source: Y. N. Kulichkov and V. D. Kalachapov, "Analysis of Production: Economic Activities of Enterprises of the Defense Branches of Industry under the Conditions of the Conversion of Military Production," *Voprosy Ekonomiki i Konversii*, no. 1 (1994): 3–8; translated in *JPRS-UMA* 94-038, pp. 22–25.

FIGURE 2.2

CHANGING SHARE OF DEFENSE ORDERS
PERCENTAGE OF TOTAL VOLUME OF DEFENSE ENTERPRISE OUTPUT GOING TO DEFENSE RELATED PRODUCTION

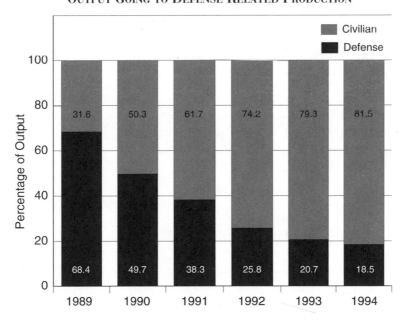

Source: Y. N. Kulichkov and V. D. Kalachapov, "Analysis of Production."

Much of the good news here can be attributed to the dramatic decline in armaments production in the defense sector. It is often difficult to comprehend how much weapons procurement has been reduced since the Soviet era without considering specific weapons programs. For example, between 1973 and 1982 the Soviet government procured on average 614 combat aircraft annually.[50] Annual procurement declined gradually from 700 in 1988, to 575 in 1990. Thereafter, it dropped off drastically.[51] According to one account, in 1994 Russian defense plants may have produced only 17 combat aircraft for the state.[52] Providing the backbone of Soviet military power, 3,500 tanks were built in 1988. But only 20 were

Figure 2.3

Russian/Soviet Combat Aircraft Procurement
Fighters and Fighter-Bombers Produced for State Orders

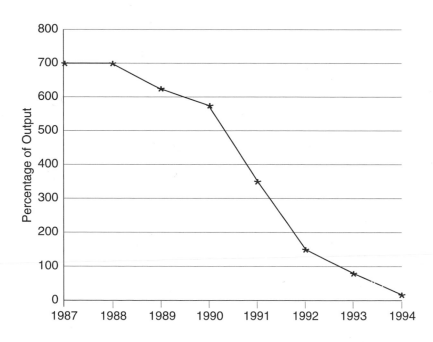

Source: Randall Forsberg and Jonathan Cohen, "Issues andChoices in Arms Production and Trade," Table 12.1; Peter Almquist, "Soviet/Russian Procurement Database"; and Aleksey Shulunov, "K chemu vedyet byudzhetnaya strategiya pravitel'stva."

ordered by the state in 1992.[53] The USSR produced approximately 1,900 infantry fighting vehicles and armored personnel carriers in 1991. After having built 1,000 in 1992, Russia produced only 300 of these vehicles in 1993.[54] Figures 2.3 and 2.4 depict the reductions in actual production of tanks and combat aircraft. Given the Russian government's financial prognosis, funds for any increases in weapons procurement in the near and medium term will be extremely difficult to come by.

The negative side of this story is that the apparent success of the defense industries in increasing their civilian output is chimerical. Although the mix of civil and military production in the defense industries has

FIGURE 2.4
RUSSIAN/SOVIET TANK PROCUREMENT
PRODUCTION FOR STATE ORDERS

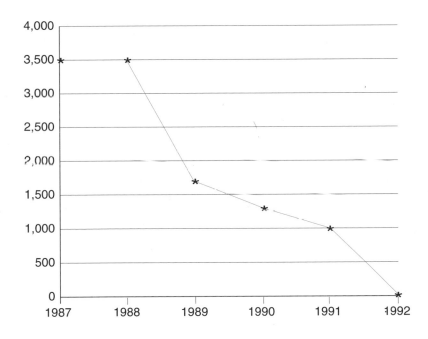

Source: Peter Almquist, "Soviet/Russian Procurement Database," Marina Chernuka andVyacheslav Terekhov, Interfax; and Aleksey Shulunov, "K chemu vedyat byudzhetnaya strategiya pravitel'stva."

swung heavily to the nondefense side, in recent years actual output of both types of goods has been *declining*. While the volume of all types of goods churned out by the defense industries has declined by more than 60 percent between 1991 and 1994, the output of civilian goods at defense plants decreased as well, by nearly one-half during this period.[55] Even civil products that were already manufactured at defense enterprises before reform were affected by the decline (see Figure 2.5). Therefore, civilian production increased its share only because it dropped at a considerably lesser rate than defense production. There are few indications that this falloff has reached its nadir.[56]

FIGURE 2.5

THE CHANGE IN DEFENSE SECTOR OUTPUT VOLUMES
(AS A PERCENTAGE OF 1991 LEVELS)

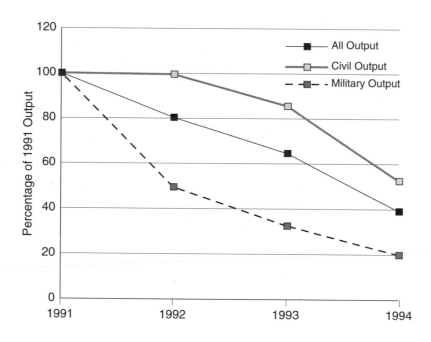

Source: Vitaliy Y.Vitebskiy, head of the main directorate of information and statistics of Goskomoboronprom, "VPK: Itogi 1994 goda" (The MIC: 1994 Results), mimeo, January 20, 1995.

BRAIN DRAIN

Perhaps more important, there has been an enormous outflow of personnel from the defense industries into new jobs elsewhere in the economy. Although "brain drain" is a phrase that usually provokes concern, in most cases involving purely domestic transfers in Russia, the phenomenon represents effective conversion as the most innovative and entrepreneurial engineers and workers in the defense complex migrate to new opportunities in the civilian economy.[57] Most of these workers have gone into private commercial work, in small firms and organizations that are completely new to the Russian economy.[58] In one example of this activity in the defense city of Perm', 120 workers left their jobs in defense enterprises to form a successful new firm that produces furniture for the Russian consumer market.[59]

It is difficult to quantify the exact scale of this brain drain because estimates of the size of defense industry employment vary widely, there is a substantial amount of hidden unemployment in large state enterprises, and since 1993 layoffs of workers have become fairly widespread but not well reported.[60] Yet a number of observers estimate that the current size of the defense industry labor force is 3–4.5 million people.[61] If accurate, this figure demonstrates that as many as half of all defense industry employees may have left their jobs in the past five years. The estimate is compatible with the results of case studies conducted by Russian economist Ksenya Gonchar. Gonchar found that most of the enterprises she analyzed had lost up to half of their workforce since the late 1980s. In most cases, workers left willingly because of low pay in their defense jobs.[62]

REPROFILING

Throughout the three periods of conversion in the Soviet Union and Russia, there have been few cases of success in the full reprofiling of existing defense facilities. It has proved extremely difficult for most defense enterprises to redirect their efforts to civilian production that is profitable and can support the entire workforce as formerly constituted. Where it has occurred in a limited way, success in reprofiling appears to take place for highly idiosyncratic reasons: some managers can make all the right choices and still fail while others may stumble upon a project that turns out quite serendipitously to be a moneymaker. Most often, a successful reprofiler possesses some manufacturing skill or process that could be directed toward the one area in the Russian economy that has flourished in the transition environment—the extractive industries. Perm' Motors, a jet engine manufacturer, has had some success in offering reworked engines as pipeline pumps to the gas and oil industries.[63] An Omsk tank factory was able to develop excavators and dredges on the chassis of its existing tractor/tank design.[64]

More often, however, enterprise reprofiling attempts look like terrible failures, typically a result of foolish choices: in selecting a product to design and manufacture, most defense enterprise managers are guilty of a supply-push rather than a demand-pull approach. They are much more likely to choose to manufacture an item based solely on consideration of the equipment and experience they have on hand than to find something that has real market demand and redevelop their facilities to meet it.

As a consequence, many enterprises have gone to considerable expense in developing an initial run of a product, only to find that it is not competitive on the market or has no demand at all. For instance, a Perm' defense enterprise decided to use its aging car parts production facility as the basis for creating an entirely newly designed automobile. Unfortunately, the prototype, being an amalgam of old designs and materials, was not even competitive with other Russian-manufactured vehicles, much less Western cars.[65] Another group of enterprises announced that they would use their remote-sensing technologies to locate logs that have sunk in Siberian rivers, raise them, and dry them out with microwaves, believing that the Russian logging industry would somehow find this process more economical than cutting down more trees.[66] A materials research institute tried to use its experience in powder metallurgy for fashioning toys. One resulting product was a toy rabbit that was made of titanium—an extremely expensive metal—that would cost approximately $1,000.[67]

Oddly enough, the existence of established civilian production lines in defense enterprises has not necessarily helped them in conversion. Given the structural and organizational limitations of today's Russian enterprises, Western investors in Russia often argue that it is preferable to "green-field"—to build a completely new facility—rather than work within existing plant facilities.[68] This argument is repeatedly borne out in practice. On first glance, the electronics and radio operations of the defense complex ought to have a relatively easy time making the transition to the civil-commercial market. Yet of all the defense industries the current slump in production is hitting these two sectors hardest.[69] One explanation may be the underdeveloped state of Russian high-technology civilian industries. Although the products of this sector are "mature," they are simply not competitive with foreign-produced goods that are now widely available in Russia. The electronics industry in particular has lagged considerably behind the West in terms of technology in recent decades and is now badly in need of major investment for modernization.[70] Another problem is that the electronics industry has been less successful than others in securing credits from the Russian government.[71]

In some cases, even adept reprofiling entails considerable pain and disappointment. The Velta plant in Perm' has benefited from being one of the biggest producers of bicycles in the former Soviet Union; when it lost much of its defense orders it was able to shift energies to an existing civilian production focus that could take advantage of an established system of suppliers. Nonetheless, the company has still lost or fired nearly half of its original workforce.[72]

Moreover, defense enterprises today must make do without most of their former privileges. They now confront the same economic constraints as do civilian industries. Few of their former customers have any money. Many potential new customers in the more dynamic part of the economy would prefer to buy abroad.[73] As a consequence, many traditional consumers of capital goods (a specialization of the defense industry) are experiencing a cash crunch. The agricultural sector, for example, has long been a major consumer of defense-industry-produced tractors, combines, and other heavy equipment. Tank plants like the Kirovskiy Zavod in St. Petersburg formerly turned out several thousand tractors per year but today find little demand for their civil output. Kirovskiy Zavod periodically has had to shut down and send its workers home on forced leave without pay.[74] In the case of medical equipment, for which there is large demand in Russia, numerous defense enterprises have recognized and acted on the need. Yet the medical industry is financially poor, so translating demand into revenue is fairly difficult.

THE NEGLECTED ASPECT OF CONVERSION:
INDUSTRY AND ENTERPRISE RESTRUCTURING

Although plant reprofiling efforts have been a substantial failure, perhaps the bigger disappointment and greater concern in the long term is the minimal amount of restructuring that has occurred within and among the enterprises of the former defense industrial ministries. Ideally, pressure from privatization, market reform, and conversion by others would spur defense managers to restructure their enterprises, selling off and breaking down into private firms that are financially self-sustaining and ultimately profitable. However, neither the huge cuts in defense procurement resources, the elimination of the centralized economy's command mechanisms, the initiation of privatization in the defense complex, the use of credits to encourage plant conversion, nor the attractiveness of the burgeoning consumer market have succeeded in transforming the majority of defense enterprises. The actual structure of the defense sector today strongly resembles that of its Soviet-era predecessor. Remarkably, virtually all of the Soviet-era defense enterprises continue to exist. Even in an environment characterized by widespread insolvency, there have not been any bankruptcies. Perhaps equally striking, essentially the same corps of directors is running these enterprises. Despite the onset of privatization and laws ordering that plant managers be elected by their labor collectives, as many as four out of five defense enterprise directors are still in office. Since the August 1991 coup, perhaps as little as 5 percent of enterprise directors have retired or been replaced per year.[75] None of this would be troubling if defense managers and their enterprises were adapting to new conditions in the economy. If they were demonstrating willingness to restructure and downsize their enterprises, establish new commercial links with new suppliers and customers, seek out new profitable civil production, and cease demanding subsidies from the state, the continuation of established management structures would not matter.

Yet by and large, defense managers and the workers who remain are doing few of these things. The vast majority of defense managers are actively resisting. Nearly a quarter of them reportedly were still refusing to take any steps toward conversion as late as November 1993.[76] Managers generally resist downsizing their labor forces, even if there is no work for them. Many of them stifle the dynamic or entrepreneurial sections of their enterprises in order to support the parts that clearly have no use in the market economy. And despite privatization, most Soviet-era defense managers have succeeded in gaining de facto control, if not legal ownership, over their enterprises.

Therefore, instead of providing salvation for the civil economy, as Gorbachev and others hoped, the defense complex exerts a continuing drag on economic reform and recovery. Most defense enterprises have little hope of sustainability in the new economic conditions. Given the collapse of state defense orders and the virtual certainty that future armaments production requirements will be several degrees of magnitude less than during the Soviet period, few can count on rescue via the military. A Ministry of Defense industrial base plan noted that only 220 of the existing enterprises would be essential for Russian security.[77] Defense managers will nonetheless continue to press their case for assistance from Moscow in the form of subsidized credits, exemptions from taxes, and so forth. Although they can hardly dictate their terms to the political system, they are a lobby to which the president, prime minister, and opposition politicians periodically appeal in attempting to outmaneuver each other. The price of these appeals, unfortunately, is often exacted in measures that run contrary to the larger goals of reform in the Russian economy.

Beginning in 1993, because of financial shortfalls many defense enterprises had to delay payment of salaries to their workers by as much as three months. In an environment of high inflation these delays proved especially costly for workers. Many enterprises also shortened their workweeks to four days for lack of work.[78] As their financial situation continues to deteriorate, the measures have become more drastic. Some enterprises began locking their doors and sending their workers home on extended leaves of absence without pay. A Russian government study found that during the first quarter of 1994 almost two-thirds of the surveyed defense enterprises were operating under an abbreviated schedule or were on the verge of shutting down.[79] By 1994, moreover, many defense managers had to go against their strongest instincts and began to fire workers outright. The same study found that approximately 80 percent of the enterprises surveyed expected to reduce their labor size during that year.[80]

No enterprise is immune from economic hardship in the current system. Even defense manufacturers that are deemed by the state to be critical national security assets are experiencing a tremendous financial squeeze. For example, in 1992 the Russian government decided to concentrate all of its submarine orders in the armaments complex of the northern city of Severodvinsk. The city was hailed by the Ministry of Defense as one of the cornerstones of current and future Russian military might. Yet in September 1994 all Severodvinsk enterprises were forced to shut down for several days when the local energy supplier cut off their heat and power. It turned out that because the local factories had not paid 70 billion rubles in energy bills, the energy company could not buy any fuel oil.[81]

Without radical restructuring and downsizing of defense enterprises, insolvency is almost certain to persist for the majority of plants, design bureaus, and research institutes. As currently constituted, Russian defense enterprises simply cannot be competitive in a market environment without huge amounts of defense orders. The Sokol Plant in Nizhniy Novgorod demonstrates the enormous excess capacity that currently bedevils these enterprises. A producer of MiG aircraft, the Sokol plant possesses the capacity to manufacture one hundred MiGs per year. Yet it received state orders for fifteen aircraft in 1993, and only two in 1994.[82] It is hard to imagine how Sokol's management can make up for this lost business. In another case, the Yuriy Gagarin plant in the Far East has benefited from substantial Chinese purchases of its Sukhoy fighter aircraft. The revenues from these sales, however, have not been enough to save the Gagarin enterprise. In September 1994 its management sent 70 percent of the labor force home on a forced leave through to the new year.[83]

In virtually all of the cases where efforts towards conversion (narrowly defined) or arms exports have been successful, the resulting production does not come close to making up for the loss of defense work at these plants. One defense enterprise formed a joint venture with Polaroid to produce cameras in its plant, but the operation supports only thirty employees out of the many thousands in its workforce. Similarly, a defense plant formed a joint venture with a German firm to produce aluminum wheels for the world market. This joint venture employs only one hundred employees out of ten thousand.[84] NPO Impuls in Moscow found products that were in demand in the Russian market—including an electronic bill (money) counter, a fiber optics television system, and camcorders—but still had to scale back its workforce by more than one-half.[85]

CHAPTER 3

WHY GOVERNMENT POLICY HAS FAILED

The failures of enterprise reprofiling and sectoral/firm restructuring in the Russian defense sector are partly the result of the basic problems of demilitarization confronted by all the former cold war competitors. Yet there are still more important causes of failure that are unique to the Russian effort. Conversion and restructuring in Russia have foundered on the twin obstacles of ineffective, often misguided government policy and considerable resistance from defense enterprise managers. Throughout the conversion period in the Soviet Union and Russia, the government has either adopted faulty strategies or when pursuing a sensible course has been too weak to implement thorough reform in the defense sector. Government policies have also had the perhaps unintended effect of strengthening the hand of the existing corps of enterprise directors, as Chapter 4 will further examine.

Part of the reason that so little has changed in the defense sector is governmental ineffectuality.[1] The transformation of the Stalinist institutions of the Soviet Union into those of a pluralist Russian state have dramatically limited the effectiveness of the government in carrying out policy. To some extent, the Russian government has had other, considerable concerns that have distracted it from the issues of the defense complex. Indeed, in a country with internal ethnic strife that threatens the state's unity, widespread conflicts on its borders, and periodic constitutional crises, relatively longer-term problems such as restructuring the defense sector often take a back burner. Coupled with internal bureaucratic divisions, these conditions create an environment in which policy initiatives promoting conversion are often schizophrenic and generally have little practical impact on developments.

51

A Government at Odds Makes for Policy Chaos

People who decry the gridlock in U.S. government would be in for a shock if they were to look at the situation in Russia. In Moscow there is no gridlock. Rather, on bad days there can be five new laws or decrees issued, some of which are contradictory and few of which are obeyed.

Although the policymaking process in Moscow has become somewhat less conflictual since the forceful disbanding of the Supreme Soviet in 1993, it is still often characterized by chaos instead of coherence. Beyond the pulling and hauling typical of competitive bureaucracies, the Russian policymaking process appears to have no rules. Decrees are occasionally issued by aides to the president in his name but without his knowledge. The government at times issues decrees despite the opposition of the president. The new legislative branch—the Duma and the Federation Council—in the meantime is still getting accustomed to its proper role. Further complicating matters, many of the initiatives churned out by Moscow are totally ignored by regional governments and the enterprises. As a consequence of all the miscommunication and cross-purposes, the government can stumble into armed conflicts like that with the separatist Chechen region without consulting with the legislative branch or, for that matter, many of the relevant ministries.[2]

Defense industry policy is no different. Although the legislatures do not play much of a role, strife within the executive branch more than makes up for their absence. Each of the organizations described below often undertakes measures implementing defense conversion without coordinating with other bureaucracies. The result is a policymaking process characterized by contradictory initiatives.

Within the Russian government there is one big advocate of the defense industries: the State Committee for the Defense Branches of Industry (*Goskomoboronprom*). Incorporating within it many of the functions of the old branch ministries and the defunct Military Industrial Commission, *Goskomoboronprom* has generally attempted to reassert the formula of a centrally directed military-industrial complex. It has sought to minimize the number of defense enterprises that are subject to privatization. Not surprisingly, *Goskomoboronprom* has consistently been an advocate of high levels of financial support—whether in the form of conversion credits or military procurement orders—for defense enterprises.

Allied with *Goskomoboronprom* have been a number of stalwart conservative organizations in the Russian government. The Federal

Counterintelligence Committee (FSK)—the successor to the KGB—during 1993–94 charged in increasingly hysterical tones that the West was attempting to spy on the Russian defense industries by means of joint ventures and business cooperation.[3] Similarly, the Federation Procurator's office has strongly criticized reformers in the government for permitting the privatization of "vital" parts of Russia's research and production base.[4]

The Ministry of Defense has had a more complex relationship with the defense industries, gradually turning from opponent to champion. Denied control over industry throughout the Soviet period, the ministry has sought to take advantage of the transformation in Russia to seize administrative and financial control over all aspects of the defense sector. Initially the new Russian Ministry of Defense was active in promoting a reorganization and streamlining of the defense complex that would have resulted in focusing government support on approximately 220 key enterprises, allowing the remainder to privatize and support themselves.[5] Indeed, the Ministry carried out this policy to some extent by concentrating its procurement orders on a smaller number of enterprises.[6] However, by the winter of 1993-94 ministry officials were increasingly sounding like representatives of Goskomoboronprom. The ministry reportedly began issuing orders for armaments production well in excess of its financial authority.[7] In 1994 and 1995 debates over the size of the defense budget, furthermore, Defense Ministry officials stridently—albeit unsuccessfully—argued for a larger appropriation in order to support financially suffering enterprises.

More firmly on the side of reform stands the State Committee for the Management of State Property (GKI). After ignoring the defense complex during the early phases of privatization, the GKI since 1993 has pushed to eradicate the last elements of enterprise privileges. Under director Anatoliy Chubays and his reform successor, Sergey Belayev, the GKI has sought to minimize the number of defense enterprises that are officially barred from privatizing.[8] Furthermore, it has sought to open up the enterprises to private shareholders, even going so far as to permit foreign ownership of most defense companies.[9]

Allied with the GKI is the Ministry of Finance (MinFin), which has consistently sought to minimize governmental support for defense enterprises. In fact, according to defense industry advocates, during 1993 MinFin often delayed its release of authorized payments to defense enterprises for work on state orders in order to limit inflation and balance the government's accounts.[10] Since the Russian Central

Bank was subordinated to the executive branch in the fall of 1993, the government has more or less hewed to MinFin's policy on minimizing industrial subsidies.

In the middle of the bureaucratic fight stand Prime Minister Chernomyrdin and, to a lesser extent, President Yeltsin. Chernomyrdin, whose background is in the energy industries, appears to be the less friendly of the two in his approach toward the defense managers. Apparently, he perceives them to be an obstacle to his economic program and a competitor with the energy sector for limited state subsidies. However, both officials have been somewhat mercurial in their handling of the defense industrialists, often playing a double game of public expressions of support and offers of political and economic favors while undermining the defense complex generally by pursuing a moderately conservative fiscal and monetary policy. For example, the government has continued to grant wage concessions, privatization exceptions, export support, and relatively small subsidies to defense enterprises. In a typical case, President Yeltsin reportedly set up a special organization for oil exporting that would divert all of its proceeds to the defense industries.[11] In another decree, Chernomyrdin ordered that no Russian enterprises could use foreign credits to purchase imported equipment without first ascertaining from Goskomoboronprom, the Ministry of Atomic Energy, or the Russian Space Agency that the defense complex could not provide the product.[12] Yet each of these measures appears short term, avoiding any ongoing government expenditures to rejuvenate the defense sector.

THE WEAKNESS OF THE RUSSIAN STATE

Not only is the Russian government internally divided, it is also remarkably weak. It has been one of the profound ironies of the Soviet/Russian revolution that as senior officials have sought to transform society, politics, and the economic system, they have had to dismantle the very means by which they could readily influence events in their country. In contrast to the regimes of Brezhnev and his predecessors, the Russian government today has very little power—either by coercion or inducement—over local governments, enterprises, or any other institutions.

As a consequence, reformers increasingly have found themselves with limited tools to implement their policies. In the Russian system today, money is one of the only sources of real influence, and the Russian government has little to spare. As the economic crisis has intensified, the government can marshal ever fewer resources to carry out even its minimal programs. The main problem has been a disastrous shortfall in tax revenues. Because of deception and the difficulty of keeping track of new entrants in the economy, as much as 40 percent of all economic activity may occur outside the view of tax inspectors.[13] According to foreign policy analyst Sergey Rogov, Russia's federal government may have received only 56 percent of its expected tax revenues in 1994. As a result, the government could fulfill only a fraction of its budgetary obligations.[14] In the case of the defense industries, the government may have provided only 65 percent of its budgeted funds for 1994.[15]

The situation is even worse for regional (oblast) and local governments. From the point of view of the city hall or regional capital, Moscow seems to be wealthy. These lower levels of government are even more strapped for money, so they, too, have limited influence over enterprises. In terms of military-industrial policy, they have even less clout than in other realms because of the persistence of centralization—perceived, if not real—in defense industry organization and budgeting. Defense managers still look to Moscow almost exclusively, unless the local or regional government somehow has money to offer. In fact, because local governments depend on the health of their homegrown industry for a tax base, their primary role in such affairs appears to be as advocates to the center for local defense enterprises.

FAULTY GOVERNMENT STRATEGY

The problem with the Russian government's policy throughout the 1992–95 period is that it did not go far enough. During Gaydar's tenure, in particular, reformers relied primarily on macroeconomic instruments to encourage adaptation by defense enterprises. The logic was that the cutoff of procurement orders and state subsidized credits alone would spur directors to convert and restructure their enterprises. This logic ignored the reality that defense enterprises were far from being market-type firms and that their directors would not respond in economically rational ways. Furthermore, Gaydar's description of his government as "kamikaze" in mission suggested to defense enterprise managers that if they just held out, Gaydar and his policies would eventually go away and they could return to their old ways of state subsidies.[16] It turned out that the directors were right. When the government resumed providing subsidized credits to enterprises, it in effect was rewarding those that had not taken any entrepreneurial risks.[17]

Later, after Chernomyrdin's ascendancy, the Russian government began to implement more thorough reform at the enterprise level, primarily through privatization. The problem, however, has been inconsistency and reluctance to carry sectoral and enterprise restructuring measures to their logical conclusion. Instead, the government has permitted widespread exemptions to privatization and has continued to release subsidized credits. Part of the reason for this hesitation has been political pressure from the defense industrial lobby. Arguably more important, however, has been the government's fear of causing unemployment. Although Chernomyrdin has stressed the need for radical revamping of defense enterprises, customarily he quickly adds the caveat that workers should not lose their jobs as a consequence.[18]

The conversion strategy of the Russian government appears all along to have been based on a faulty assumption, reflecting fear of the so-called Weimar problem: to implement restructuring in defense industry too quickly could result in extreme socioeconomic dislocation. This, in turn, would produce mass demonstrations and disorder in Russian politics. On the evidence, these concerns seem largely to be unfounded. Fears of disastrous unemployment may be fueled by defense managers and their supporters in an effort to secure increased state support. In contrast to the mining sectors, defense industry labor unions are poorly developed and cannot credibly threaten to the block their production since no one wants it anyway. Although defense industry advocates periodically threaten nationwide strikes, the turnout for these labor "disturbances" has consistently been low. It is, after all, difficult to generate a large demonstration when all of the workers are on forced leaves of absence. In fact, some strike activity appears to be organized by the managers themselves in order to promote their demands for state subsidies.

Furthermore, unemployment appears not to be a worry to the people who should fear it most—those involved in local government. In interviews with oblast and city administration officials in the highly defense-dependent region of Perm', even with considerable prompting all would express only minimal concerns over defense industry unemployment. The local economy in Perm' is expanding dramatically, and most workers who leave local defense enterprises find new jobs in it.[19] The situation appears to be similar in other defense industry regions. The main exception to this local dynamism is the single-enterprise, closed cities of the nuclear weapons complex. These ten or so cities do not realistically have any prospects for growth now that their raison d'etre has been overtaken by events. Thus, they will continue to require direct assistance from the state.

THE PROBLEM OF LIMITED PRIVATIZATION

The biggest failure of the Russian government has been its reluctance to carry out a thorough privatization of most defense enterprises. Although the government has initiated privatization, the restricted nature of its approach has had unintended negative consequences, serving to increase the power of enterprise directors with respect to both the state and their workers. The result is that the enterprise directors have achieved all of the autonomy of owners but none of the responsibility.

The goal of reformers in the Russian government seeking privatization originally was to encourage the development of market-oriented firms. By transferring ownership of state enterprises to private hands, reformers aimed to create effective corporate governance of these organizations.[20] Enterprise management would be held accountable to the new owners, whose primary motivation would be profit. The profit motive, so the logic went, would drive the board of directors and management to restructure in order to eliminate inefficient operations and develop those that could compete in the market. If management were unwilling or unsuccessful at these tasks, the owners—like any Western corporate board—presumably would replace them. These positive developments would be reinforced with the establishment of hard-budget constraints on the firms' activities.[21]

Yet by and large neither effective corporate governance nor hard-budget constraints have been achieved. Instead, privatization has mostly taken an insider form where the enterprise management has gained de facto, if not legal, property rights over the enterprise. This insider privatization is the result of two developments perhaps not anticipated by the designers of the privatization program. Labor has almost blindly backed management. The managers, however, appear to have effectively minimized labor's voice in enterprise governance. By resisting layoffs managers have satisfied labor's primary concern—job security. Moreover, the managers appear to have succeeded in persuading labor that the state is the source of all their problems: the delays in their salaries, the lack of useful work to perform, and, when they occur, layoffs. Labor in the defense enterprises continues to be very poorly organized. The old Soviet trade unions served more as transmission belts for the state than as representatives of labor. Those that have survived the transition and many of the new ones that have developed are even now either unrepresentative or ineffective, or both.[22] Thus, rather than pressure management, workers have even sold their shares to the managers.[23]

In addition, managers have thus far have blocked effective outside ownership of enterprise shares. Most defense enterprises privatized according to the option allowing the majority of shares in a particular enterprise to be owned by its workers and management. In the vast majority of cases, managers have convinced workers to support them in resisting external investors by playing on fears that outsiders will demand widespread layoffs.[24] Although the privatization program calls for those shares not purchased by the management or the worker collective—49 percent in the case of enterprises restructured under the "second option"—to be sold off to private investors, in the defense sphere these remaining shares are rarely offered for public auction.[25] This defense industry privilege appears to be the result of lobbying by Goskomoboronprom, which holds any unsold shares. The managers are usually satisfied with the arrangement because Goskomoboronprom typically transfers its authority to them.

Managers have also benefited from indirect state support that discourages outside ownership. The August 1993 presidential decree governing defense industry privatization and subsequent legislation specify that the manager of any enterprise producing for defense must be certified by the state.[26] As a consequence, any group of investors seeking to take over ownership faces the prospect that it will not be permitted to replace the current management. Furthermore, the state's retention of the "golden share" of ownership in many defense enterprises makes potential investors anxious that their capital could be lost at the whim of state bureaucrats.[27] These fears appear to be wholly warranted, as the state evidently does not want to cede its voice in even those enterprises that become fully private. In the case of the Vympel Interstate Joint Stock Corporation, a multienterprise aerospace organization headquartered in Moscow, Goskomoboronprom blocked the privatization process until the management agreed to place its chairman, Viktor Glukhikh, on the new corporate board.[28]

Hard-Budget Constraints

Initially, some defense managers were reluctant to privatize for fear that they would not be able to count on state support. However, managers have since learned that the likelihood of subsidy for their enterprises is not related to their ownership status. Those that the state deems important—for security or political reasons—continue to receive preferential credit regardless.[29] Nor are hard-budget constraints likely to be imposed in the near future. In his July 1994 speech on economic policy, Prime Minister Chernomyrdin noted that while the government plans to replace the management in some enterprises that are in default, it would not impose more than a few token bankruptcies.[30]

NEBULOUS PROPERTY RIGHTS AND THE AUTONOMY OF THE MANAGER

Michael McFaul argues that of the three classic forms of property rights—use, profit from use, and transfer—the only one not yet acquired by the managers is transfer.[31] In most cases it appears that legal aspects of ownership have little bearing on what defense managers can or cannot do. For example, the general director of an aviation design bureau explained that the controlling packet of shares in his organization was the packet that he owned, regardless of its size. He noted that he could hypothetically sell a foreign buyer up to 75 percent of the shares in his design bureau without sacrificing his personal control.[32]

The nebulous nature of real property rights has become a major obstacle to restructuring in the defense sector. Increasingly, defense enterprise managers are buying and selling shares in each others' enterprises, forming new "corporate" groups that unite enterprises but do not control them, as well as swapping stakes with the joint-stock companies within their own enterprises. In an extreme example, the Leninets Holding Company, a St. Petersburg enterprise, has a byzantine network of cross-ownership. The holding company management holds the controlling packet of shares—37 percent—in each of the joint-stock companies and organizations within it, in addition to part ownership in larger amalgamations. Each of the suborganizations and joint-stock companies within Leninets also holds shares in the holding company.[33] In another case, the director of an aviation institute, GosNIIAS, explained that his institute has gained controlling shares in a number of multienterprise joint-stock companies that are its customers.[34]

At first glance this behavior might be interpreted as a sign of vigorous reorganization of the Russian market. On closer inspection, however, these increasingly complex webs of cross-ownership appear to be designed primarily to reinforce the existing directors and their partners. By owning shares in traditional suppliers and customers, an enterprise director is gaining partial insurance that outside investors or the state will not come in and throw out the management with which the director has long-established personal ties. Similarly, the enterprise director's position is reinforced by the transferring or selling of shares to partners in other enterprises.

These webs of ownership are marriages of convenience for defense enterprises. Because the managers of partner enterprises share interests, cross-ownership seems to have little impact on the day-to-day operation of enterprises.[35] It is doubtful that an enterprise manager would ever attempt to use his leverage in another enterprise in a hostile way. Yet enterprises can still fall back on these arrangements to defend themselves against unwanted intervention by the state or private investors.[36] Exchange of shares and cross-ownership, therefore, are serving to entrench existing managers as well as reinforce their traditional supplier and customer relationships.

Not surprisingly, these webs of cross-ownership have been deemed highly illegal. A November 1992 government regulation reportedly banned outright the cross-ownership of subsidiaries and holding companies.[37] But like much else in the Russian defense complex, what the government commands is not necessarily what the enterprises do.

CHAPTER 4

THE MANAGERS

G iven the failings of state policy and the liberating effects of privatization, the managers of defense enterprises have emerged as the key players in the Russian conversion drama. Managers' attitudes as well as their economic and political strategies have become central in determining the course of enterprise reprofiling and restructuring.

Perhaps the biggest surprise in the Russian defense industries in recent years is not that restructuring and conversion have failed to progress substantially, nor even that the enterprises have avoided closure or the replacement of their managers. Rather, it is that, despite the radical changes in the economic and political environment, the basic behavior of defense enterprise managers continues to be economically dysfunctional. Although they have taken advantage of new opportunities offered by the commercial world, too many continue to look to the state, not the market, for their survival. As a result, most managers pursue conservative strategies aimed at maintaining the existing structure and size of their enterprises, as well as their own positions within them.

THE CULTURE OF THE SOVIET ENTERPRISE MANAGER AND THE PERSISTENCE OF MEMORY

A number of Western analysts have developed a clear picture of the attitudes and interests of the typical director of a state enterprise in a Soviet-type economy, and how they differ from those of a manager of a firm in a more free-market-type system.[1] Especially in the defense sector, the Soviet economic system bred a great deal of conservatism in the enterprise manager's approach to the job. Defense enterprises and design bureaus received fairly stable orders; changes were usually incremental, and production or design tasks once completed were usually followed by orders of a similar nature and scale. Managers operated in an environment where resources were extremely scarce and supply uncertainties were constant. Faced with the overriding importance of meeting the targets of their economic plan, enterprise managers were socialized under these conditions to become extremely risk-averse. As a consequence, they tended to hoard resources and labor, skimped on product quality, and were reluctant to innovate in their manufacturing processes and designs if such changes might upset their ability to deliver on time.[2]

Though the Soviet economic model entailed extensive state involvement, its governing plan was more the product of a series of bargains between enterprises, regional governments, and the center than any simple command issued from bureaucrats in Moscow.[3] In contrast to the managers of market-oriented Western firms, Soviet defense managers typically engaged in a great deal of noncompetitive "rent seeking."[4] Broadly defined, rent seeking behavior occurs when individual efforts to maximize value generate social waste rather than social surplus. Rent, like profit, is that part of a payment to an owner of resources over and above what those resources could command in any alternative use—revenues in excess of opportunity cost. In a free market, because the existence of a profit for a particular product or service will always draw new competitors, the system naturally drives the price down and eliminates the profit. Rents differ from profits in that they are not competed away. Thus they reflect a diversion of value from consumers generally to the favored rent seeker, with a net loss to the societal welfare in the process.[5]

Noncompetitive rents result from market failure, for instance, monopoly, or government actions such as the provision of licenses, quotas, permits, franchise assignments, or subsidies. Import tariffs result in rents for the protected industry but losses for the economy at large. Although all firms—market-type or otherwise—engage in some degree of rent seeking, it typically is just one relatively small aspect of their behavior.[6] However, as rent seeking takes on a larger role in the firm's strategy, it increasingly crowds out activities that are productive from the standpoint of the larger economy and society.

The Soviet defense manager was perhaps the ultimate rent seeker, accruing rents through privileged access to resources and various forms of government support, especially the awarding of prestigious military contracts.[7] These were enhanced, of course, by the implicit knowledge that the government would never permit the enterprise to go bankrupt. It followed that the defense manager would benefit more from cultivating personal contacts in the bureaucracy than from improving the productivity of the enterprise.[8]

Thus, while Soviet defense managers developed few entrepreneurial skills useful for operating in market economy, they still had to be extremely effective at political and bureaucratic maneuvering in order to prosper within the system. Successful defense enterprise managers were shrewd operators in securing resources and minimizing demands put upon them. One of their main skills became the ability to conceal their enterprises' assets while avoiding demands for increased output from central planners.[9] These characteristics served them well when they had to protect themselves from the disorder of the political and economic transition.

The other remarkable aspect of the Soviet defense manager was in his (they were invariably male) role as veritable lord over the fiefdom of his enterprise, its workers, and the social support infrastructure. Most defense managers clearly developed a great attachment to the prestigious role they played in their community. Many viewed themselves as proudly paternal in their relationship with their workforce, feeling some obligation to provide for their "extended family."[10] While these feelings were honest, like most parents the managers expected to be treated with respect and deference by their workers in return.

Finally, perhaps even more than elsewhere in the world, the corporate culture of Soviet defense managers tended to emphasize product performance and high technology at the expense of affordability and customer satisfaction. Here again the Soviet system played a determining role in the managers' socialization. The current Russian first deputy minister of defense, Andrey Kokoshin, complains that in the Soviet system the dominant incentives led to development of weapons that were extremely impressive on paper—say, a Mach-3 fighter—without much concern for how they would function in the field.[11] Because of their privileged access to resources, Soviet defense managers did not have any reason to concern themselves with cost. Moreover, since industry tended to dominate over the uniformed military in the procurement and design of weapons, defense managers typically were not held accountable to their customers.[162]

THE CORPORATE CULTURE OF THE DEFENSE MANAGER TODAY

As the transition in Russia has progressed and defense managers have adapted their behavior to new conditions, many of the core values of their traditional corporate culture persist. This is especially the case for their inclination to be rent seekers. Although they are happy to make money commercially where they can, most managers look to the state rather than the market for business and support.

Most defense managers appear unable to make the psychological changes necessary to operate independently in a free market environment. The majority continue to demonstrate a profound lack of faith in, and a serious misunderstanding of, the workings of a market economy. While most defense directors accept the need to find new civil/commercial production tasks, many resist establishing new supplier and customer ties. Instead, they stress the value and need to maintain their position in the economy vis-à-vis their traditional enterprise partners. In explaining their views most managers recite a mantra extolling "the technological chain." They warn that if one link—one organization—within this chain were removed, Russia would lose a precious resource.[13] Moreover, having turned out the finest products in the Soviet Union, defense managers honestly cannot understand why they lack orders. Many are bewildered as to why the West and their own government do not recognize their importance and value to today's Russian economy.

Typically, Russian defense managers perceive themselves to be uniquely distinct from their market counterparts. Consequently, many of them scoff at the idea of Western experts telling them how to run their enterprises. One design bureau manager who is very interested in joint-venture projects with Western partners argued that while foreign businesspeople are better than Russians at "tactical business concerns," the Russian manager is clearly the superior "strategic" thinker. He elaborated that foreign businesspeople are too concerned with tactical issues—like legal matters—at the expense of longer-range, more fundamental considerations. It turned out that his vision of "strategic" issues includes the essential importance of the government and Western investors supporting his "technological chain."[14]

It is not surprising, therefore, that defense managers experience serious difficulties whenever they foray into the business world, either with Russian or foreign customers. A defense industry critic writing in *Nezavisimaya Gazeta* highlighted the cultural barriers that constrain defense managers in the marketplace:

> It turns out that enterprises entering into negotiations with a potential investor are ignoring his interests entirely and operating in the old way, as though with their own ministry. You give us something and that is the end of it. Many enterprises have doctors and candidates of sciences on the staff,

including economists, *but they are not accustomed to considering the commercial prospects for expensive, long-term projects* and do not know how to compile a convincing business plan for the investor. [emphasis by the author][15]

Another critic complains that "if one listens to the directors, he gets the impression that the military industrial complex is still full of vitality and that it is only necessary for the state to give it some money and then the colossus will get moving again. . . ."[16]

Defense managers are not necessarily opposed to personal enrichment through commerce. In fact, they engage in a variety of creative strategies to make money by exploiting their enterprises' assets. But the typical defense manager appears to be more concerned with maintaining the status quo ante—the shape and size of his organization, his own power within it, etc.—than with adopting potentially more lucrative commercial or restructuring strategies that would require a shake-up. For example, managers often resist the temptation to spin off the most successful elements in their enterprises into private operations, even if they own them.[17] Instead, they prefer to use their successful operations to subsidize struggling ones.

MANAGERIAL STRATEGIES

What impact does the persistence of Soviet-type, rent-seeking managerial culture have on defense enterprise behavior? As a general rule, it translates into conservative, economically myopic actions. Although the need for radical restructuring, downsizing, and reorientation of enterprises has become quite clear, defense managers generally have adopted a very cautious strategy of minimizing changes to their enterprise structure and sticking to the trading partners and the types of production tasks with which they have had extensive prior experience. In general, their goal appears to be survival, or subsistence.

Conversion Goals. The typical defense manager has a very specific agenda of priorities and needs in preparing to convert for civilian production. First and foremost, the enterprise must survive as currently constituted. Second, whatever project the enterprise converts to should be of a technological level comparable to its prior defense output. Reflecting a pride in the prestige of their work, managers are often appalled by stories of former defense engineers using their talents to make consumer goods like bicycles. Only when the manager can give his employees no other work will he consider such "lesser" tasks. Perhaps as important, and in a number of ways linked to the first priority, defense enterprise managers seek to convert to products that will be in demand on foreign markets. In their minds, export work represents the surest source of hard currency and is infinitely preferable to doing work for the government. This is another reason to make the most of their high-technology skills and processes—which they perceive to be globally in demand—in reaching out to the consumer markets.

A good example of managerial attitudes can be found in Moscow's NPO Mashinostroyeniya, a recipient of conversion assistance from the United States. NPO Mashinostroyeniya is a defense enterprise with a long history of developing satellites, rockets, and sea-launched cruise missiles. Its management favored an earth imaging satellite, "Almaz," as its central conversion project, despite the overcrowding of suppliers in this global market. Some members of the management were angry, therefore, when the United States decided to finance instead a program at the enterprise that would develop a cola-producing facility for the Russian consumer market.[18]

In order to carry out their ambitions, virtually all managers complain that they are in dire need of investment. They loudly demand financial support first of all from the Russian government. When this method fails, they have used other approaches to force the state to help them. Similarly, many managers pursue foreign partners for joint ventures that will fund their conversion work.

Hoarding Labor. One of the central tenets of the conservative defense industry strategy has been a resistance to downsizing and the release of labor. Although many enterprises were forced to begin laying off workers in late 1993, the practice appears to be an absolute last resort. Enterprise directors prefer to reduce their plants' operating tempo—shortening the working week of their labor force or sending them home on forced leave for months at a time—rather than fire workers.

In the defense director's mind, there are a number of reasons to keep a labor force well in excess of the available work. One is historical experience. In the Soviet system, the greatest failure of an enterprise would have been an inability to meet its planned production targets. Failure would result in the forfeiture of the manager's bonus and a stain on his record.[19] But worker productivity was poor, the supply of labor nationwide was tight from the 1970s onward, and one never knew when plan targets might be increased in the middle of the year.[20] As a consequence, it was axiomatic that enterprise managers would hoard resources and labor in order to provide themselves with cushioning "just in case." Defense directors have not abandoned this tendency, even if the original reasoning has been overtaken by events.

Today there are several new reasons to hoard labor. A large labor force translates into political capital for the rent-seeking manager. When requesting or demanding subsidies from the federation or regional government, the likelihood that an employer's voice will be heard is often directly related to the number of people it can claim to represent. Directors of large enterprises constantly warn that their plants must be supported or else terrible unemployment will be the result. As discussed previously, such arguments work: it appears that very large enterprises—10,000 or more employees—receive the vast bulk of government financial assistance.[21]

Furthermore, given the progressive structure of wage taxes, managers can reduce their tax burden by paying a larger number of workers a lower wage.[22] Thus, they are likely to keep "dead souls" on the official rolls—even if they have left for better opportunities—and not pay them, in order to grant higher salaries to staff that are, in fact, working.

The effect of these phenomena is to make most defense enterprises resemble ghost towns of the American West. A visitor entering the gate of the average Russian defense enterprise today is usually ushered up to the office of the general director. Judging from this office, life at the enterprise is normal and the staff often works late. But if the visitor ventures out into the plant's facilities, a decidedly different picture emerges. Virtually all shops and production lines lie dormant, and there are few workers in sight. Occasionally one might find a particular facility where a shop manager and a few close staff are developing a new project or working on a defense order. But these are a tiny minority.[23]

Production Inertia. The vast reduction in state orders for armaments was not accompanied by a genuine shrinkage of the defense sector. What are all those enterprises doing? Through late 1993, many of them were doing what they had always done, producing weapons even if there were no orders for them. Taking the first quarter of 1993 as an example, the government allocated only 6.5 billion rubles ($13.1 million) worth of orders, but industry produced 20 billion rubles ($40.4 million) worth of defense output. Seemingly, many managers ordered their plants to continue defense work with the belief that the state defense planners had a made a foolish mistake that they would soon reverse; that excess weapons could be sold for hard currency on the world market; that the government would probably pay for the product regardless of whether it was needed; or all three of these in combination.

The defense manager's decision was not necessarily arrived at with lengthy deliberation. Having been socialized in the command system, when the economic transformation began most factory directors were quite literally at sea in terms of knowing what to expect or what would be demanded of them. It is not surprising, therefore, that their behavior was irrational in appearance and economic fact. An illustration is provided by the story of a tank plant in Omsk. Its director, Sali Aleksandrovich Katyk, received state orders—and presumably financing—for only 5 T-80 tanks in 1992. Yet he chose to produce 155 tanks that year. His reasoning was that conversion should not entail a reduction of defense output. If he must "convert," his notion of doing so was to keep making tanks and sell them abroad. Unfortunately, Katyk did not have a foreign buyer, so the tanks he produced were mothballed. When a reporter made the mistake of opining that Russia does not need any more tanks, Sali Aleksandrovich became irate:

> Who told you that? Who knows generally how many weapons we need and what sort? Is it five tanks a year for Russia—how did they [the government] arrive at that? Possibly we have an officially approved military doctrine or plan for modernizing the armed forces or a general plan for national security? I know nothing about that. I don't understand why the Russian Army needed five tanks from Omsk and not 25.[24]

Unfortunately, Sali Aleksandrovich was by no means the exception in producing well in excess of state orders. In 1992, despite cuts in procurement orders by 68 percent, there was only a 38 percent decline in actual defense production.[25] Tank makers, for example, manufactured twenty-six times the number of tanks that the Ministry of Defense had requested.[26]

In fact, both civilian and defense enterprises initially attempted to continue with their former production tasks without any idea of who would eventually buy their output. In the defense sector, enterprise managers were able to proceed in part through the use of their existing stocks of materials, and in part by tapping into their mobilization reserves that were required by law to be preserved in case of national emergency.[27] Some managers themselves decided that it was a national emergency and that excess weapons production was in order.

Interenterprise Debts. The lion's share of resources for this excess production, however, was provided through lending between enterprise partners. Faced with a shortage of working capital and unable to borrow from banks, enterprise managers across the spectrum of manufacturing continued to supply one another as before. Instead of paying, however, each provided the others with goods on credit. Because the managers were trading with long-established partners, they were willing to extend credit regardless of the risk that it would not be paid back.[28] The enterprises would forward their output to the next factory in the supply chain until the end producer/final assembly facility, which usually would end up just storing the output.

This interenterprise lending created a host of problems for the health and stability of the economy as well as the reform process. It was driving the production of output for which there was no customer to pay the bills. Between January and July 1992 the level of interenterprise debt rose from 4 percent to 25–40 percent of gross domestic product. These debts undermined the Russian Federation budget. Because no cash was switching hands, value-added tax revenues dropped. Furthermore, interenterprise lending became an obstacle to privatization; the huge debts that enterprises were running up made them very unattractive targets for private investors. Finally, as the web of debts grew larger and more complex, there was an increasing risk that the failure of a few enterprises could cause a cascade effect in which scores of others would also collapse, including potentially healthy enterprises.[29] Although this was a problem throughout the Russian economy, the opportunity costs of defense interenterprise lending were especially high. In the current environment defense output represents a substantial negative net value to the economy. (According to one estimate, the resources that go into the average weapon are worth twice as much as the end product.)[30]

In order to alleviate these problems, the Russian government sought on a number of occasions to enforce discipline in enterprise transactions. Its efforts were consistently undermined, however, by the Russian Central Bank, which periodically injected subsidized credits into the system in order to allow enterprises to settle their debts with one another.[31] This permitted them to continue amassing new arrears in the belief that the government would not let them fail. As a result, despite the government's elimination of all the debts in summer 1992 and its subsequent efforts at restraining the practice, by January 1993 the level of interenterprise arrears had again reached 20 percent of GDP.[32] The Central Bank measures to reduce debts, meanwhile, were fueling inflation.

The cycle of new arrears, fresh credits, and increasing inflation persisted until fall 1993. In the aftermath of the October turmoil, the

Chernomyrdin government made sure the new constitution enshrined Central Bank accountability to the executive branch, not the new parliament. Although the government has wavered in its tight-money policy, many enterprises have become uncertain about the reliability of future state subsidies. Thus, the new policy has had the benefit of gradually forcing most enterprises to insist on cash or in-kind payments before the delivery of goods. By 1994 most defense enterprises had scaled back substantially the amount of output that they produced in excess of state orders.

Although the Russian Federation government has fought interenterprise lending and overproduction, at times it too has been a culprit. In 1992, the Ministry of Foreign Economic Relations anticipated export orders for Russian armaments worth $3.1 billion. With this forecast in hand, the ministry issued orders to a large number of enterprises to produce several billions worth of weapons. However, when real export sales that year amounted only to $1.1 billion, the ministry did not reimburse manufacturers for their surplus inventory, and many of these defense enterprises were left with large bills and no customers for their products.[33]

As interenterprise lending has diminished, delays in the disbursement of government funds have become the principal source of debt in the system. Partly because the Ministry of Defense issued orders in excess of its budget authority, partly because the Ministry of Finance delayed the disbursement of state payments, and in part as a result of shortfalls in tax revenues, by February 1995 the government reportedly owed roughly 3.2 trillion rubles ($80.2 million) to the defense industries for arms procurement and research.[34]

Manager Financial Creativity. The defense managers have exploited their enterprise assets in a variety of ways either for personal enrichment or to support their enterprises. For example, many enterprises possess extremely valuable real estate. At the St. Petersburg Rubin submarine design bureau, the director has built a hotel where the staff is comprised of former designers and workers from the plant. NPO Mashinostroyeniya in Moscow has a less innovative but still profitable use of some of its facilities. The management is using its dormant test facility for sea-launched cruise missiles as a warehouse for storing Japanese television sets.[35] Following their experience with cooperatives during the Gorbachev period, enterprise managers reportedly channel orders to small companies in which they hold the commanding shares. For example, the Russian government's head prosecutor complained that the general director of the Zvezda state defense enterprise had illegally transferred several million rubles from the cash office of his enterprise to three firms whose cofounders are his sons and wife.[36]

Defense managers have also been very creative in their accounting. Even if an enterprise is profitable, the manager will seek to adjust the books to reflect a loss in order to avoid the state's profit tax. Only a foolish manager would ever show a profit.[37] In a play on an old Soviet aphorism, one design bureau director joked, "They [the government] pretend to tax us [the managers], and we pretend to pay them."[38] Beyond manipulating the accounts, most defense enterprises organized their own banks during 1992-93. By controlling a bank, the enterprise director could profit from high inflation rates: upon receiving state conversion credits, the manager could withhold the funds from workers and put them to other uses. After a delay in which the real value of the money declined, wages would then be released.[39]

Managerial Aversion to Restructuring. On the face of it, many defense enterprises are undergoing some internal restructuring. For example, most have developed "marketing" and "conversion" departments. But closer inspection suggests that these departments are still little more than names on doors. Tarja Cronberg notes that a number of Perm' defense enterprises created marketing departments simply by renaming their planning departments.[40] In a Moscow aviation systems institute, the director of marketing explained that his job entailed only promoting existing products, not researching demand. And at another Moscow region aerospace enterprise in early 1994, the director of the conversion department confessed that the department consisted of him alone, that he had just been appointed, and that he had no idea of what he was going to do.[41]

Social Support Assets. Defense managers similarly have been resistant to the idea of reducing their social support functions. Although the enterprise's responsibilities for providing housing, kindergartens, health facilities, and other social services for its workers imposes a high overhead cost, many managers nonetheless view these functions as assets. In competing for workers they cannot offer the high salaries available in the emerging private sector. But they can offer extensive social benefits that the typical firm cannot—and would not—think of providing. In a number of cases, these "vital" assets include luxuries such as resorts in the Crimea.[42] Michael McFaul suggests that managers use these assets as a means of maintaining paternal control over their workforces and encouraging worker passivity.[43]

The interests of the defense managers and the Russian government sharply diverge on the issue of social support functions. Not surprisingly, the same functions that the manager looks on as assets, the Russian government perceives as exorbitant. Deputy Defense Minister Kokoshin, who is responsible for arms procurement, complains that the cash-strapped Ministry of Defense should not have to pay for these functions.[44] Prime Minister Chernomyrdin has stressed the importance of separating the social welfare sphere from enterprises by transferring responsibility for such services to local government.[45]

Spin-offs. The conservatism of managers toward restructuring is nowhere more apparent than in spinning off successful operations within their enterprises. One of the most promising developments in the Russian defense industries is the growth within the structure of existing enterprises of operations based upon a department, shop, or facility that has a particularly entrepreneurial manager or useful technology or process that has some demand in the outside market. There is no way to quantify just how many exist in the Russian defense sector today, but it appears there are numerous potential spin-offs within every defense enterprise.[46]

The growth of these subunits is indirectly encouraged by managers. By early 1994 most defense managers were decentralizing decisionmaking to departments, suborganizations, and shops. In many cases enterprise heads began to permit differentiation in salaries in order to reward those shops that went out and generated orders.[47] This strategy provided an effective incentive to lower-level managers and department directors to innovate and find new applications for their products and services.

To an extent, this is an extremely effective means for increasing the flexibility of enterprises and tapping into the various talents contained within them. Yet taken alone this step appears to be wholly inadequate for the survival of the enterprise as currently constituted. Under conditions of dramatically reduced defense expenditures some departments inevitably will lack business: some assets will be impossible to convert; others will lack competitive technologies. For the most part, however, directors are attempting to maintain all the departments within their enterprises. They apparently view successful departments as a means to support the entire enterprise rather than operations that should be encouraged to stand on their own. As a consequence, they assess high overhead charges to the most adaptable in order to subsidize the less successful facilities.[48] This, of course, serves to stifle whatever promise these subunits possess.

Because it is difficult enough for a business to operate in the Russian economy without the added burden of high overhead charges, many forward-looking departments would prefer to spin themselves off from the larger enterprise and go it alone. The problem is that they are in many ways beholden to the enterprise director. Housed within the larger enterprise, they depend on it for facilities, electricity, heat, and other supplies. They often cannot do anything without the manager's approval. This lack of independence was made plain in a discussion of finances with a joint-stock company within the Leninets Holding Company in St. Petersburg, in which the author was warned to keep his voice down because the general director of the holding company might be bugging the meeting room.[49] In another, more extreme case, a department director was forced to haul all of the equipment for his spin-off out onto the front lawn, where he set up his operation literally outside the parent enterprise.[50]

A logical compromise would be to permit the department to spin off if the manager were guaranteed a share in its profits or service on its board of directors. Yet this approach is rarely adopted. For most managers, the survival of the entire enterprise—and all the perquisites that accompany it—seems to be a greater value than personal (monetary) wealth.[51]

The Russian legal system, furthermore, strongly supports the senior management in disputes with potential spin-offs. By law, structural subunits may not be separated from privatized enterprises if together they constitute a single technological complex.[52] The enterprise manager appears to have enormous latitude in defining what is part of his "technological complex." For example, the director of NPO Mashinostroyeniya reportedly declared the kindergartens in his enterprise to be subcontractors for defense production in order to keep them under his control. Another manager of a Urals research institute noted that in the past he permitted successful operations to spin off because he did not believe he had any right to stop them. Since he became aware of his legal rights, however, he simply fires the director of any department that is agitating for independence.[53]

THE MANAGERS' PREFERENCE: FINANCIAL-INDUSTRIAL GROUPS

Although many defense directors have been pressured into measures such as decentralizing decisionmaking authority or laying off some workers, these measures are regarded as tactical responses to urgent needs. The directors' hearts clearly point them in the opposite direction: toward increasing their size through amalgamation with other enterprises, banks, and investment companies.

Among members of the League of Defense Producing Enterprises, the defense industry lobby that claims to represent 700 enterprises, the idea du jour—rather than streamlining—is the financial-industrial group (*finansovaya promyshlennaya grupa,* or FPG).[54] As the directors generally describe it, the FPG is an alliance of a number of interdependent enterprises, design bureaus, and research institutes. At the center of the group is a bank that is devoted to providing each of the members with their capital requirements. The virtues of this system would be the internalization of financing as well as the minimization of uncertainties with respect to suppliers. The FPG would emphasize high-technology products primarily for the export market.

Although there may be areas of the economy in which this type of organization makes sense, in general the FPG model does a better job reinforcing further the place of existing directors than facilitating a free market. Proponents of the FPG point to the success of diversified industry amalgamations such as the Daewoo concern in South Korea. Yet the idea also bears a striking resemblance the old Soviet model of the multienterprise scientific production association (NPO), except that FPGs would be larger in size and self-financing.

In fact, the concept of the financial-industrial group incorporates many of the traditional wishes of the defense managers. For one, the FPG is huge and generally autarkical in character. The entire "technological chain" between partner enterprises can be incorporated within it, insulating managers from the pressures of the larger economy. Planning, rather than competition, clearly is one of the dominant themes. As one FPG supporter in the government explains it, "What is needed are groups of enterprises linked together financially and technologically, exercising precise planning of joint work. . . ." The same aide explained that the export emphasis would save Russian enterprises from painful competition with each other in the internal market.[55] In organizing the financial-industrial groups, the directors stress that they will need subsidies from the federation government. In order to protect them during their "infant industry" phase, moreover, they will probably call for tariff barriers and export assistance.[56]

Defense industry officials and their advocates in the government argue that a number of these organizations already exist. For example, Kokoshin points to FPGs such as that based on the Omsk Polyot plant, the Ilyushin design bureau, and a Voronezh manufacturing plant, as well as one that incorporates the Yakovlev design bureau and the Saratov aviation plant.[57] Numerous new groups register with the government every month.

Yet such organizations appear thus far to be nothing more than formal expressions of existing enterprise networks. The legal standing of the groups and the interaction of enterprises within them are literally being made up as they go along.[58] A big failing of the FPG idea so far has been that commercial banks, seeing much better returns elsewhere in the economy, refuse to get involved. Naturally, commercial bankers would prefer to take over a defense enterprise outright rather than join in an alliance that will support the existing directors.[59]

ARMS EXPORTS AS PANACEA[60]

One of the most worrisome aspects of conversion in recent years has been the increasing enamoration of defense managers and the Russian government with arms exports as the cure for their financial woes. As the financial crisis in industry and government has grown more acute, leaders from both spheres have come to view armaments as among the few products that will earn much-needed hard currency. The proponents of arms exports advance arguments that range from arms sales' usefulness as a means for financing enterprise conversion activities to their being a long-term source of revenue that should be cultivated in its own right.

There are a number of problems with the logic behind these arguments, most of all in the excessively optimistic assessment of Russia's export potential. Arms export proponents generally cite the Soviet Union's exports of upward of $20 billion per year of armaments in the early 1980s, claiming that Russia essentially "surrendered" this market to Western arms exporters. Given the high quality and cheap price of Russian-made weapons, they reason, it would take little effort to win these markets back.

These estimates ignore two important facts. First, the Soviet Union on average was paid for only a quarter of its arms exports. The remainder were transferred for political reasons or with extremely favorable credit arrangements.[61] Second, the demand for arms on the international market today is almost half of what it was in the mid-1980s (see Figure 4.1). Although the United States has dramatically increased its share of the overall market, it too has experienced an absolute decline in the value of its arms exports. All of the world's leading weapons sellers have experienced similar declines. Thus, the arms export boosters' projections are wildly off the mark. Although Russia may make modest gains in terms of the overall value of its arms exports, it is less clear if the country will see commensurate increases in real hard currency revenues. In 1994, Russia only earned approximately $1.7 billion in arms export revenues, well short of expectations.[62] In fact, many of Russia's recent arms export successes that optimists point to are much less than meets the eye. Some deals have been composed in large part of barter arrangements.[63] Other agreements to ship high-performance aircraft were in fact arms-for-debt swaps to cover Moscow's foreign repayment obligations.[64]

If disappointing arms export advocates was the only consequence of inflated expectations, there would be little cause for concern. But the prospect of greater arms exports appears to have led many defense managers to hold off on restructuring or at least reprofiling their enterprises. As long as they believe that they will be able to make money with their

FIGURE 4.1

VALUES OF GLOBAL EXPORTS
MAJOR CONVENTIONAL WEAPONS, 1984–93

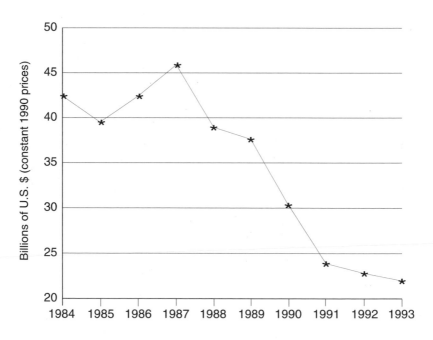

Source: SIPRI Yearbook 1994, Stockholm International Peace Research Institute, table 13B.2.

existing production, they are likely to forgo real restructuring or adjustment to market conditions. Furthermore, as the hopes for arms export success inevitably are not met, there will be increased pressure on the Russian government to permit sales to states under international sanctions or otherwise considered to be unsavory. Russia has already caused considerable consternation in the West by transferring diesel submarines and civilian nuclear reactors to Iran. Moreover, Russian diplomatic efforts to lift the embargo against Iraq seem in part motivated by the desire to renew former arms ties.

GROUNDS FOR OPTIMISM

Despite intense resistance by managers, by the end of 1994 it appeared that market forces were finally compelling some defense enterprises to adapt in constructive ways. Although the government was still providing large and very large defense enterprises with support, many smaller and medium-sized enterprises were increasingly being left to fend for themselves. Overall, the level of production for which there was no demand and interenterprise debt had stabilized at an acceptably low level as the flow of government-subsidized credits slowed.

These conditions have forced a number of defense managers to come to terms with the market in a more aggressive way than previously. As the futility of simply easing their operating tempo became more obvious, managers began to lay off redundant labor, with the hope that they could retain their best specialists and workers.[65] Similarly, many managers found themselves confronted with the unavoidable need to shed some of their social support assets, or they demanded assistance from local government. For instance, in early 1993 Perm' defense enterprises began to refuse to pay for the heating, water, and electricity for their apartments, obliging the city government to pick up the cost.[66] By 1994 this behavior appeared to be widespread among both reformist managers and rent seekers. Only the heavily subsidized large enterprises could afford to retain much of their social support infrastructure.[67]

Although no defense enterprise bankruptcies have yet occurred, these developments indicate that when enterprise managers are confronted with hard-budget constraints, they will in fact respond appropriately. It remains to be seen how far the managers will be willing to go: How will they restructure, will it be effective, and will it be enough? According to the estimates of Yevgeniy Kuznetsov, only 10 percent of the current corps of defense managers have become true entrepreneurs.

Generally speaking, these managers are in charge of medium-sized enterprises and are optimistic about their chances of survival—even of
making profits—in the market economy. Instead of any particular
privileges from the government, these managers seek only law, order,
and stability.[68]

Indeed, one of the most promising aspects of reform is actually a
nondevelopment: the lack of social and political tension in defense industrial regions. Despite several years of dire warnings from defense advocates, social and political disturbances, like the oft-predicted famines
of the perestroika era, never materialized. This relative stability should
provide those working for conversion with a great deal of latitude in all
but the most defense-dependent regions.

The immediate goals for defense conversion and restructuring
efforts in Russia, therefore, should be to reinforce and assist entrepreneurial directors and provide stronger incentives to those who still resist the
new ways of thinking about business organization and management
practices. Ideally, managers who persist in opposing reform will be replaced
by those who can prosper in a market environment.

CHAPTER 5

POLICY PRESCRIPTIONS FOR
FACILITATING CONVERSION IN RUSSIA

There are four vital, interrelated questions confronting Russia as it carries out defense industry conversion and restructuring.

1.   How to restructure the defense sector to create economic organizations that are self-sustaining—that is, creating profit-making firms that possess a "total business capability";

2.   How to instill in managers an understanding of business operations under market conditions;

3.   How to find new investment for these firms in order to stimulate civilian manufacturing; and

4.   How to provide an improved social safety net, a modernized economic infrastructure, and new employment opportunities to cushion the transition.

The experience of Soviet and Russian conversion attempts over much of the past decade vividly illustrates that the tasks these questions entail are extremely demanding. A successful effort will require a significant political and policy commitment from the Russian government. Yet in all likelihood this will not be sufficient. Russia will require substantial assistance from the West in a number of areas where it cannot adequately help itself, particularly marketing experience and investment. New and embryonic Russian firms would benefit from direct, practical training or exposure to modern techniques of market research, presentation, and positioning in a practical forum. Furthermore, given the dearth of financial resources in Russia, new start-ups or firms undergoing restructuring almost always require some targeted investment. Although these roadblocks are endemic throughout the Russian system, the West has a special security interest in removing those obstructing change in the defense sector. Western conversion assistance, therefore, should aim primarily toward helping to create new, civilian-oriented firms making use of human and capital resources from the defense sector, and retraining managers to operate under market conditions.

Fortunately, a relatively small amount of support from the U.S. government can go a long way toward solving Russia's problems; conversion does not necessarily require a massive aid program like the Marshall Plan. Instead, seed capital provided by the Washington can be used to spur American private industry into forming business partnerships with the most promising ventures arising out of the Russian defense establishment. These partnerships can provide a long-term, self-sustaining mechanism for conversion. Although a variety of mechanisms and strategies can—and should—be used by Western specialists to help Russia convert and restructure its defense sector, all efforts should be based on a common set of principles and goals.

CONVERSION GOALS

EMPHASIZE CONVERSION AS BROADLY DEFINED

The thrust of foreign assistance for Russian conversion should be directed primarily at the broad (macroeconomic) and intermediate (sectoral/firm restructuring) levels. The prospects for enterprise reprofiling of defense production lines to civilian/commercial output would not be very promising under any circumstances, and with economic conditions what they are in Russia today, the outlook is decidedly poor. Besides, any assistance for reprofiling runs the risk that entrenched managers will continue to eschew necessary restructuring and reform of their organization.

Therefore, foreign assistance should avoid promoting a policy of saving existing defense enterprises as an end in itself. Clearly, there are too many defense enterprises in the Russian economy, most of them saddled with fundamental flaws in organization that seriously impair their ability to survive in the market. The aim should be to free the valuable assets—human and material—held by the defense sector and concede that little can be done productively with the remainder.

CREATE NEW FIRMS THROUGH DOWNSIZING AND RESTRUCTURING

The most direct means of achieving the conversion of the Russian defense sector would be through downsizing and restructuring enterprises into self-sustaining firms. In each case the goal should be to create new firms on the basis of potentially successful departments within the enterprise. Such departments should be spun off, freeing them from the prohibitive overhead and other constraints imposed by the management of the larger enterprise. Thus they can take better advantage of their own specialization and a more rational division of labor.

These small spin-offs are the most dynamic and innovative feature of the Russian economy today, forming a class of market-responsive firms that have been sorely lacking until now. To the extent that the Russian government or foreign assistance helps any of these new firms to succeed, it will demonstrate to old managers and new entrepreneurs alike that this is the way to go forward.

CREATE A "TOTAL BUSINESS CAPABILITY"

Virtually all new firms and old enterprises in Russia need to develop what is known as a "total business capability."[1] This includes aspects of business that are taken for granted by companies in a free market economy: an understanding of the market for the goods that they choose to produce, designing products for cost-efficiency, a reasonable plan for how to deliver wares to market, and the ability to provide support after sale. Russian firms must completely reorient themselves toward a "demand-pull" approach—one in which product costs, specifications, and design are determined by the market.

INSTILLING ENTREPRENEURIALISM

One goal of foreign assistance should be to help create a new class of entrepreneurial managers. Whether they are reformed enterprise directors or are part of the new generation, the management of new and converting enterprises should be instilled with a culture of entrepreneurship, characterized by profit-seeking, risk-taking, innovation, and, most importantly, an orientation toward the market rather than the state. Since most conversion attempts inevitably will end in failure, the most durable contribution that Western assistance can make is helping to create a new breed of entrepreneurs in Russia.

FINDING INVESTMENT: HELP PRIVATE INDUSTRY LEAD THE WAY

Realistically speaking, the conversion and restructuring of the Russian defense sector cannot depend upon a massive aid program like the Marshall Plan. Neither the Western governments nor international lenders possess resources sufficient to bail out the many Russian defense enterprises and their spin-offs. Moreover, providing large sums of money to the defense industries is a disincentive to change.

U.S. and Western private industry, however, have both the resources and the means to use them effectively. Successful business cooperation between Western industry and new Russian firms ultimately will provide far more of value to the Russian economy than any aid program could ever hope to do.[2] Private industry can make more efficient use of investment than could a government aid program. Entrepreneurs can assess risks and sound out projects and adopt flexible strategies to make the most of them in ways for which government bureaucrats just are not positioned. Moreover, private enterprise generally fares better when it is not bound by the restrictions that accompany government programs.

FINDING NEW PRODUCTS: EMPHASIZE PROJECTS THAT WILL HELP RUSSIA

Although the selection of a new product that has market potential and is compatible with a firm's labor and capital capabilities is a highly individual process, Russian and American policymakers should follow a few rules in choosing projects to support. On balance, Russian firms should be pursuing a strategy that targets the burgeoning demand for quality consumer and capital goods in Russia rather than export-led growth. Most defense enterprise managers would prefer production for export—either of civilian or defense goods. In their view, this is the most effective strategy to exploit their technologies and can also generate hard currency. However, this strategy is exceedingly optimistic and ignores the needs of Russian consumers and industry. Generally, the technologies that the defense managers extol are either widely available in the world market or will necessitate years of development to find real commercial applications. In the meantime, managers will continue to depend upon state subsidies. Their ambitions represent yet another manifestation of a "supply-push" approach to conversion.

A more pragmatic and helpful approach would be to focus on developing domestic markets. Increasingly, Russian consumers rely on expensive, imported consumer goods because the quality of homegrown products historically has been so poor.[3] Aided by tremendous, pent-up demand throughout Russia today, many firms emerging out of the defense complex likely will find sizable markets for household goods within their own cities and regions. There is substantial reason to believe that after the initial attraction of imported goods wears off, most consumers will be glad to "buy Russian." Moreover, there should be substantial opportunities for production in Russia of lower-tech goods, whose markets, reportedly, are not nearly as saturated as in the West.[4]

Firms that are not equipped to manufacture competitive consumer products should opt for capital goods. Capital goods are something that many of the small and medium-sized enterprises in the defense sector can make quite capably. As Russian industry restructures and begins to expand again, moreover, the demand for these goods will be substantial. As in the case of consumer goods, Russian firms frequently will be able to find customers locally, eliminating the need to rely on the creaky national infrastructure or state-run transport to ship their products long distances.

INTEGRATE AND CONCENTRATE ASSISTANCE PROGRAMS

Because so many of Russia's problems are interrelated, their successful resolution requires efforts that integrate a variety of support programs. For example, directed conversion assistance will make little impact if newly converted firms cannot count on long-term loans from Russian banks or if they cannot purchase property in their locality. There already exists a wide variety of programs in the United States and Europe supporting Russia and the other former Soviet states in their transition to market economies. As a general principle, these programs would benefit if they were coordinated. Although such coordination often proves difficult even among the various U.S. agencies, the United States should make an effort to integrate its programs with those of European Union and the European Bank for Reconstruction and Development.

Western assistance would probably improve its effectiveness by concentrating on a few cities that have demonstrated a reformist inclination. By focusing on areas where assistance is welcome, the West might manage to overcome obstacles that, when viewed Russia-wide, appear insurmountable. If successful, these "model cities" could have influence on market adaptation elsewhere that magnified the amount of assistance. Ideally, support would be targeted on the somewhat neglected cities and regions beyond Moscow and St. Petersburg—where much Western investment and assistance is currently concentrated.

DO NOT OVERSELL THE PROGRAM

Finally, it is essential that any foreign conversion assistance program not be oversold either to Russia or to the U.S. Congress and public.

Converting and restructuring the Russian defense sector will take a long time—at least a decade and perhaps more. While U.S. assistance may be necessary, it alone will not do the job. Furthermore, macroeconomic redirecting of resources and sectoral/firm overhaul are not the kind of phenomena whose success can be easily measured and displayed on a briefing chart. The real value of conversion assistance will be through demonstration: a few successes should provide the momentum for Russian and Western entrepreneurs to join in, creating a multiplier effect.

Therefore, in developing and promoting any aid program, the Clinton administration or its successors will have to emphasize to Congress and the public the long-term nature of the effort. If the program is held to a standard that demands results in one to two years, it will inevitably come up short. Alternatively, its administrators would be forced to channel their efforts toward high-publicity, low-risk goals that may not be relevant to the genuine solution.

On the Russian side, many managers in the defense sector today express bitterness that the West has ignored them and is secretly hoping that they fail. Their anger is based on the misperception that was prevalent earlier among enterprise workers and their bosses that if the East-West political conflict ended, foreign investment would come rushing in. Instead, they feel, Western aid went to paying for high-priced Western consultants or, worse, intelligence agents who have posed as businesspeople.[5] Rather than encourage this misperception any further, Russian and American organizers of any assistance program should emphasize that the directors must come to them with ideas, instead of waiting for the solutions to come knocking.

EXISTING WESTERN AID PROGRAMS

During the 1994 fiscal year the United States provided roughly $1.6 billion in aid to Russia. The U.S. Agency for International Development (AID) alone contributed $1.2 billion for programs ranging from developing securities trading facilities (such as computer networks and clearinghouses) to help with the privatization process and housing sector reform.[6]

Mechanisms for supporting U.S. investment in Russia generally include the Overseas Private Investment Corporation (OPIC) as well as the U.S. Russia Investment Fund. OPIC is a self-sustaining, independent agency of the U.S. government that promotes economic growth in developing countries by facilitating American investment. OPIC provides direct loans to small and medium-sized U.S. companies for new investment projects or the expansion of existing ones.[7] It also offers insurance for investments in developing countries to protect against a variety of political risks: political violence affecting assets or business income, expropriation without fair compensation, and inconvertibility of the local currency.[8] For financing projects in the former Soviet Union, in particular, the Clinton administration granted OPIC $1 billion of authority over the 1994–95 period. OPIC will participate with direct loans, for up to 50 percent of the total project cost for a new joint venture, and up to 75 percent of the cost of an expansion. According to OPIC president Ruth Harkin, the organization has reserved up to $500 million for financing and guaranteeing defense conversion projects in Russia involving American equity participation.[9]

The U.S. Russia Investment Fund is a private investment firm organized and initially funded by the U.S. government. The Fund operates under the general supervision of a board of directors appointed by the president and is managed by a team of financial experts selected by the board. In 1995 the Fund was provided with $440 million in grants from the U.S. Agency for International Development.

The Fund offers financing and management support in the form of equity investments, loans, technical assistance, and training to Russian enterprises, Western firms interested in pursuing opportunities in Russia, and Russian-Western joint ventures operating in Russia. The U.S. Russia Investment Fund also has a Small Business Lending Program that works through a network of Russian banks and other lending institutions to make loans to small enterprises. The only requirements for the Fund's consideration of proposals are that the client have a committed and progressive management, a coherent business plan, and real potential for growth and profit generation. In contrast to OPIC and the Demilitarization Enterprise Fund (discussed below), applicants for assistance need not have an American partner.[10]

The Nunn-Lugar Program

U.S. government initiatives directed specifically toward the defense industries primarily fall under the rubric of the Nunn-Lugar Cooperative Threat Reduction Program. Named for its initial sponsors, Senators Sam Nunn and Richard Lugar, this program was conceived as a means of assisting the four nuclear states of the former Soviet Union in dismantling their nuclear weapons, thereby stemming the dangers of proliferation of weapons of mass destruction.[11] Since 1991 Congress has authorized that $1.2 billion of the Defense Department's budget be applied to tasks such as:

- providing equipment to transport nuclear warheads from Belarus, Kazakhstan, and Ukraine to Russia for dismantlement;

- making available equipment to disassemble nuclear delivery systems in all four states;

- constructing facilities and implementing measures for the safe storage of weapons of mass destruction prior to their dismantlement;

- offering employment to scientists and engineers involved in weapons of mass destruction to minimize the risk of their emigration to outlaw states;[12] and

- devising means for the destruction of chemical and nuclear weapons.

Since fiscal year 1993 the scope of the Nunn-Lugar program has been expanded to include funds for the conversion to civilian purposes of defense industries in the post-Soviet states.[13] Conversion has since made up approximately 11 percent ($135 million) of total Nunn-Lugar planned spending.[14] The 1994 conversion portion of the Nunn-Lugar authorization comprised four distinct programs:

1. The "fast four" enterprises—a streamlined process of funding for joint ventures between U.S. companies and four selected Russian enterprises;

2. Direct aid for joint ventures between U.S. firms and an additional eighty-two enterprises;

3. The Prefabricated Housing Initiative; and

4. The Demilitarization Enterprise Fund (or the "Defense Enterprise Fund").

The "fast four" are pilot projects expediting joint ventures with targeted Russian defense enterprises. The U.S. government is providing

seed capital, approximately $20 million in all, to which the business part-
ners must add their own contributions of capital, labor, and other
resources. Washington selected the four Russian enterprises to participate
in new ventures with American business partners oriented toward
production of goods for the Russian civilian economy. These include:

- Production and bottling of soft drinks for local consumption—
  Double Cola Company of Chattanooga has teamed with NPO
  Mashinostroyeniya in a $6.1 million effort that will potentially
  employ 200 workers. The U.S. government is providing $5.1 mil-
  lion to the project;[15]

- Production of equipment for Russian dental facilities—International
  American Products of Columbia, South Carolina, has joined with
  the Leninets Holding Company in St. Petersburg to produce new
  dental chairs and support equipment for sale to Russian dental clin-
  ics. The joint venture project is valued at $3.9 million, of which
  Washington is offering $1.9 million;[16]

- Production of hearing aids for the Russian market—Hearing Aids
  International of Sommersworth, New Hampshire, has created a joint
  venture with NPO Istok, an electronics and microwave producer,
  to manufacture hearing aids. The U.S. government will contribute
  $5.66 million of the $7.4 million project;[17]

- Development of a satellite-based air traffic control system for the
  Russian Far East—Rockwell-Collins heads a team that has joined
  Russia's GosNIIAS in the development an air traffic control network for the Pacific region. Rockwell will provide the technologies
  for its global position system (GPS) receiver and traffic-alert col-
  lision avoidance system. Hughes will provide its TracView air traffic control system. GosNIIAS will develop and modify the products
  for application in Russia. The U.S. government will lay out $4.1 mil-
  lion, while the industry team will bring $600,000 of its own.[18]
  International air travel in Asia is expected to benefit a great deal
  from the resulting improved system.

The Department of Defense planned to fund the other eighty-
two enterprises involved in weapons of mass destruction in a less
expedited manner.[19] The Defense Nuclear Agency sought to provide awards
valued at $1–5 million for projects with these companies. As in the

case of the fast four, the U.S. government would only be contributing seed capital with the aim of fostering a long-term business relationship between the American and Russian partners. However, at the time of this writing, it appears that the Defense Department has decided to merge the so-called list of eighty-two into the Defense Enterprise Fund, rather than maintain it as an independent program within Nunn-Lugar.

The Prefabricated Housing Initiative includes $20 million for joint U.S.-Russian production of homes for demobilizing Russian officers from the Strategic Rocket Forces. Five Russian enterprises have been selected as candidates to twin with U.S. firms and convert part of their facilities to the production of prefabricated housing.[20] The program aims to capitalize these enterprises sufficiently so they have a high probability of succeeding in the ruble economy.

The Demilitarization (Defense) Enterprise Fund will ultimately be the primary means of American assistance in the conversion of Russian enterprises. The fund is a nonprofit organization established to provide financial support to joint business initiatives between U.S. firms and privatizing enterprises for defense conversion in Russia, Belarus, Kazakhstan, and Ukraine. Although the Fund is endowed by the Department of Defense, like the other enterprise funds, its operations are completely independent of the government. The selection of projects will be based primarily on three criteria. In order of priority, these are: Will the project be an effective means of converting defense assets? Is there a low risk of failure? Will it make money?[21]

The mandated focus of the Fund is exclusively those Russian enterprises that were formerly involved in the production of weapons of mass destruction. Its mechanisms for support include making equity investments, offering loans or grants, and providing collateral for loans.[22] As of mid-1995, the Fund had been capitalized at a level of $27 million, with another $40 million due to be allocated in October 1995.[23]

By summer 1995, the Defense Enterprise Fund was reportedly ready to make commitments amounting to close to $7 million for three projects in Russia. One of these projects would team Caterpillar, Inc., with St. Petersburg's Kirovskiy Zavod for the production of platforms for excavating equipment. The total value of the project is approximately $5 million, of which the Fund would kick in $1.8 million.[24] The ratio of Fund investment to U.S. private investment is approximately one to two. A second project teams the U.S. firm Hamilton-Standard with the Nauka joint venture to produce environmental control systems for Russian-built commercial aircraft. The DEF will purchase up to $2.75

million in equity in the joint venture. The ratio of DEF investment to other Western capital is about one to eight. Finally, the DEF plans to invest $1–2 million in a joint venture for software programming between Transcontinental Systems Development Group (TSDG) and NPO Istok.[25]

There is additionally one set of conversion efforts that does not fall under the Nunn-Lugar rubric. The Department of Energy sponsors an Industrial Partnering Program to foster cooperative work between U.S. national laboratories, American industry, and research institutes throughout the Soviet successor states. U.S. companies and Department of Energy laboratories first negotiate proposals as Cooperative Research and Development Agreements. The U.S. laboratories, in turn, negotiate subcontracts with their counterparts in Russia and the other countries.[26]

OTHER WESTERN ASSISTANCE

Of course, the United States is not alone in assisting Russian defense conversion activities. The European Union's program for Technical Assistance to the CIS (TACIS) includes a defense conversion component.[27] Since 1991, TACIS has been entrusted with the mission of assisting the former Soviet states with the transition from central planning to a market economy. Although the $650 million (510 million European currency units) program is rather modest in size, it includes programs for nuclear safety, the environment, social services, education, telecommunications, and policy advice.

TACIS will allocate approximately $23 million to defense conversion efforts over the 1994–96 period. The majority of these funds—roughly $14.5 million—will go toward programs for retraining Russian military officers. The remaining $8.5 million will assist converting defense enterprises.[28] In order to receive support, defense enterprises in the former Soviet Union submit proposals to TACIS units in their home countries. If approved, a proposal is forwarded to a TACIS team with overall responsibility and then, on an annual basis, to the European Union for approval. Once a project is selected, the EU issues a request for proposals from suitable Western partners for the Russian enterprise. The funds are awarded to the Western partner. For example, TACIS is supporting a European partnership with the Mil and Kamov helicopter design bureaus for the development of new civilian helicopters. Other projects appear less production oriented and more concerned with technical issues such as the development of market research capabilities and applied research contracts. Within Russia, TACIS is concentrating its efforts on four cities: Moscow, St. Petersburg, Tyumen, and Samara. It reportedly plans to expand its activities to Chelyabinsk, Yekaterinburg, and Perm'.

In addition to TACIS, the European Bank of Reconstruction and Development (EBRD) has sponsored a number of projects that assist defense conversion. The EBRD is a multilateral financial institution that lends and invests exclusively in the countries of Central and Eastern Europe. Capitalized with over $12 billion, the EBRD provides advice, loans, equity investments, and debt guarantees for projects that help develop the private sector, increase direct foreign investment, create and strengthen financial institutions, etc. The United States is the largest shareholder in the bank, with a 10 percent stake.[29] In one program, the EBRD provided a $40 million credit to the Baltic Shipyard in St. Petersburg for the construction of dry cargo ships ordered by a Norwegian customer.[30] The EBRD also maintains a Small Business Fund that is dedicated to supporting micro- (fewer than twenty people) and small enterprises.[31]

ASSESSING THE WESTERN PROGRAMS

The various Western programs to aid Russia are impressive in their scale, creativity, and diversity. Yet these efforts have come under increasing criticism, some of which is merited. Part of the problem has been the West's warranted eagerness to provide aid in a timely manner. U.S. and other Western aid providers appear at times to have rushed to award contracts to companies that were ill-equipped for the task at hand or that were better at consulting than implementing.[32]

On the other hand, the Nunn-Lugar program has encountered objections for not spending money fast enough. Although the Cooperative Threat Reduction program was budgeted for $1.2 billion between fiscal years 1992 and 1994, by January 1995 only approximately $480 million worth of contracts had been signed, and only $150 million of this money had actually been spent.[33] The delay proved costly to the program as congressional authority for $212 million expired and could never be spent. Some congressional critics began to complain that, after two years of implementation, the program had not dismantled a single nuclear warhead.[34]

The difficulties that Nunn-Lugar has encountered originally stemmed from organizational problems. As originally mandated by Congress, Nunn-Lugar programs were to be funded out of the defense budget, but Congress neither provided additional funds nor specified from which defense programs Nunn-Lugar monies should be subtracted. As a result, for the first two fiscal years, the Department of Defense had to identify programs within its budget that would provide Nunn-Lugar financing—a difficult task in terms of bureaucratic politics—then it had to seek specific program approval from the House and Senate appropriations committees.[35] By fiscal year 1995 the Congress and administration had addressed the problem by creating a specific Cooperative Threat Reduction program budget with earmarked funds, thus accelerating the process considerably. Thereafter, the delays in spending were for more acceptable reasons, such as difficulties in negotiating specific contract arrangements. By January 1995 the level of "proposed obligations"—the identification of specific activities to be financed—was roughly $962 million.

The primary problem on the U.S. side now appears to be obtaining adequate funding from a more skeptical Congress. Although the entire Nunn-Lugar program faces financial pressure, the future for defense industrial conversion funding may be especially troubled because it still ranks as a lesser priority. Although the initial focus on weapons of mass destruction is justified, in order to demilitarize the Russian economy over the long term the emphasis should be expanded to all types of defense enterprises. The $7.67 million that initially launched the Fund is clearly insufficient for that purpose.

The most worrisome problems for the Cooperative Threat Reduction program involve the Russian bureaucracy. In particular, the Russian Ministry of Atomic Energy and Industry (MinAtom)—the only member of the original *devyatka* that remains—has insisted on maintaining high levels of secrecy and tightly holding the reins of Nunn-Lugar monies affecting production facilities for nuclear warheads and the dismantlement of the weapons. The Ministry of Defense has also demanded greater say in the participation of Russian defense enterprises in Nunn-Lugar-sponsored joint ventures. It is not clear whether the obstacles put forth by these two ministries are a reflection of increased fears about national security and secrecy in Russia or merely the desires of aggrandizing bureaucracies to get a share of the Western aid pie.

Considering Western aid programs broadly, another problem is overlap and redundancy in missions. In addition to the Defense Enterprise Fund, which is dedicated exclusively to defense conversion, the United States has another enterprise fund and OPIC, both of which can also provide assistance to conversion projects. The European Bank for Reconstruction and Development—partly funded by the United States—also provides assistance for conversion-related projects, and the EU's

TACIS program supports conversion through enterprise partnerships and consulting arrangements for Western firms. These various programs ought to be better integrated. The main virtue would be concentration and coordination—so that all the funds and institutions do not go chasing the same projects. In particular, if conversion programs prove to be less lucrative than investment in the Russian civilian sector, it will be all the more important to maintain an investment fund dedicated exclusively to conversion. Since the United States bears the largest share of the aid burden, it logically should take the lead in pressing for greater coordination and integration.

A COOPERATIVE CONVERSION STRATEGY

What policy measures are necessary to implement the goals outlined above? Fortunately, existing assistance programs and institutions provide a valuable framework to expand upon. Arguably, defense industrial conversion in Russia will require a strategic partnership between the United States and Russia at the levels of both government and industry. Instead of a massive aid program, the partnership should respect the comparative advantages of government and private enterprise activity, employing each for what it does most effectively. While some direct assistance by the United States may be necessary for large-scale infrastructure and social support projects, the primary focus of conversion cooperation should be industrial partnerships: joint ventures between U.S. companies and Russian spin-offs. Here the respective governments need only provide the impetus and context for cooperation. Joint ventures by private enterprise should shoulder most of the burden and risk, and reap the economic benefits of this process.[36]

As a general rule, joint venture prospects initially should be identified and acted upon by the respective business communities. The willingness of American businesspeople to commit their own time and resources should be the standard by which an assistance program evaluates the merit of any proposed joint venture project. Most important of all, the prospect of a joint venture with a Western firm should spur resourceful departments within existing defense enterprises to spin themselves off and form new firms, thereby empowering reform-oriented managers. Spinning off would ensure that the efforts of the Western partners were not unintentionally supporting other, less dynamic sections of the larger defense enterprise. The partnership aspect of the program should ease the transmission of new skills from American to Russian firms.

The contributions to the joint ventures should be based on each partner's particular strengths. The Russians can contribute advanced engineers and designers, a highly educated labor force, as well as plant facilities. Western partners can provide investment in new civilian manufacturing, new technologies or production processes, and general business know-how. The profit incentive should prompt the American partners to help new Russian firms structure themselves to compete. One of the best means of transferring managerial wisdom and manufacturing skills is by having people work side by side.[37] Such joint ventures should help foster entrepreneurship in the new generation of Russian managers.

Foreign-assisted partnership efforts should eschew financial-industrial groups and those enterprises seeking to create them. Although conceptually similar organizations function effectively in some other industrialized economies, in Russia these groups usually represent restructuring in the wrong direction, toward preserving existing enterprises and their managers. Inevitably it would be extremely difficult to verify that foreign-sponsored business partnerships with these groups would not be subjected to the same problems of misallocated overhead charges that characterize enterprises and their components today. Russia already has plenty of concentration in industry. What it needs most of all now is a good dose of restructuring in a downward direction, taking advantage of the flexibility and innovation of small firms. There is no reason to oppose U.S. business becoming involved with financial-industrial groups on its own. However, the U.S. government should not offer assistance, not even indirectly.

Why would Western businesses be interested in investing in Russian defense conversion? The benefit of the industrial partnerships for the Western partners would be a share in profits and technologies, as well as access to the Russian market. American firms could benefit from exposure to advanced Russian technologies in certain fields. According to an official at Rockwell International, potentially lucrative opportunities exist in materials science, computer science, computational flow dynamics, biomedical research, artificial intelligence, and advanced sensors.[38]

A number of American firms have already entered into partnerships with Russian defense enterprises in order to profit from sales in Russia and abroad. For example, Pratt & Whitney is collaborating with the Ilyushin aviation design bureau on the new Ilyushin-96M commercial airliner. Encountering problems of reduced demand for jet engines in the West, Pratt & Whitney hopes to find new markets by supplying the engines for the Russian aircraft, which Ilyushin hopes to export. Rockwell-Collins similarly is working with the State Scientific Research Institute for Avionics Systems (GosNIIAS) on joint development of avionics for the Ilyushin airliner. The U.S. embassy in Moscow estimates that there are seventy to eighty existing or pending defense conversion joint ventures in Russia today. Together they could be worth an estimated $600 million to $800 million of investment.[39]

However, many more potential Western investors or partners have held back because of fear of the political climate or economic conditions, confusion about the law, and a variety of other concerns. The role of government, therefore, should be to create the conditions that encourage U.S.-Russian business partnerships. Both governments should take steps to reduce the concerns of prospective foreign partners while providing them with added incentive to enter the market. The Russian government must lay the legal and economic groundwork for partnerships. The U.S. government can make its contribution by providing investment insurance and seed capital—financial backing such as matching funds for initial private investment—to help companies reduce the risks of pursuing their own profit-seeking activities in Russia.

The Role of the Russian Government

Although the Russian government can contribute little in the way of investment resources for conversion and restructuring projects, its active participation in creating and maintaining the conditions for these ventures will be essential. Of course the history of Russian government policy provides little grounds for optimism. One of the primary requirements for successful partnerships is stability in the economic, political, and legal systems—a task to which the government has not proved itself equal as yet. Given the government's failures, most of the measures recommended here involve its getting out of the way more than trying to work actively for conversion.

The foremost task of the Russian government should be the acceleration of its program of macroeconomic reform and stabilization. The success or failure of large-scale conversion and restructuring will hinge most prominently upon the state of the Russian economy. If it is unstable and weak, there will likely continue to be a dearth of investment to start new businesses and those that do enter the market will find their day-to-day operating conditions to be extremely difficult. Free prices and an extended period of steady, reliable macroeconomic policy should help eliminate many of the chronic problems in the Russian economy, such as shortages and uncertainty.

The Russian government will also have to eliminate most of its subsidies to the defense industry. Although the government will probably have to continue to subsidize the largest enterprises (20,000 or more employees) because of the dangers of unemployment sparking political discord, it can and should eliminate subsidies and credits to the smaller ones. Any hint of future largess runs the risk that rent-seeking managers will continue looking to the government rather than undertaking reforms. Fiscal austerity will be an essential means to spur the rationalization and revamping of defense enterprises; by making good on the threat to allow insolvent ones to go bust, the government will be imposing the hard-budget constraints that managers have thus far avoided. Managers who continue to block restructuring and conversion can then be removed by angry shareholders or through bankruptcy proceedings. The money saved from curtailing subsidies can be more productively used to support a social safety net of unemployment insurance, local government takeovers of social services formerly controlled by the enterprises, and retraining for redundant workers.

The Russian government would clarify matters a great deal if it were to identify a limited number of defense enterprises that it deems to be critical for national security. It has taken steps in this direction, but its current list of essential enterprises is double the 220 originally specified by the Ministry of Defense. The government should return to the ministry's shorter list. Those enterprises that do not make the new short list, cut off state support, will have to find their way either on their own or through joint ventures with Western partners.

The Russian government should also reduce the restrictions on ownership of defense industrial assets. Current laws on property rights and privatization grant too much power to the directors of defense enterprises at the expense of departments and components that could effectively spin themselves off. There is nothing wrong with the Russian government maintaining restrictions on outside participation in defense enterprises that it views as critical to Russian security. But the same restrictions need not be placed on less critical enterprises. This issue must be addressed promptly because it will be extremely difficult to promote spin-offs once the directors gain full legal ownership of their enterprises.

There are a number of other legal measures that the Russian government should adopt in order to facilitate joint ventures for conversion. It should develop and enforce laws that provide strong protection of the intellectual property rights of any foreign firm and its joint ventures. Western businesses operating in Russia frequently complain about inadequate recourse against theft of ideas and designs. Often they resort to negotiating situation-specific arrangements with their Russian partners. This process, however, is time-consuming, laden with uncertainty, and probably deters many Western businesses from getting involved in the first place. Similarly, the Russian government should provide legal guarantees that foreign partners will be able to repatriate fully their earnings.

There are problems in Russia today that appear to defy resolution; nonetheless, it is difficult to imagine the long-term success of conversion, or economic reform and recovery for that matter, without their remediation. One of these is organized crime, which takes a harsh toll on all kinds of new businesses. Unfortunately, there are no obvious, short-term solutions to Russia's organized crime problem. Eventually, greater openness and a reduced state role in the economy should eliminate many of the opportunities for corruption in the system.

Another thorny issue concerns the Russian tax structure. The current byzantine system, which evolved piecemeal instead of springing from a coherent fiscal policy and includes taxes on profits, wage taxes, and a value-added tax, would strain companies' accounts if it were actually obeyed. Because it is ignored, however, it deprives the cash-strapped government of essential resources, especially at a time when local organs must take on many social responsibilities. Because it is unworkable, the tax regime encourages all sorts of corruption on the part of enterprise managers.

THE ROLE OF THE U.S. GOVERNMENT

The measures required of the U.S. government to encourage industrial cooperation are qualitatively different. In order to foster worthwhile U.S.-Russian conversion partnerships, Washington should provide American industry with inducements to lead the way. Industry will require some government backing to help overcome the initial obstacles and uncertainties of foreign investment in Russia.

Encouraging private industry to take the lead offers a number of economic and political advantages. First, the profit motive promises the best prospects for long-term success, encouraging the participants to make their projects businesslike and self-sustaining. Second, it maximizes the effectiveness of the limited resources that the U.S. Congress is willing to devote to Russian defense conversion. Third, by providing new opportunities for the American business community it will create new jobs and a domestic political constituency to maintain focus on the program's vitality over the long term.

The ideal mechanism for supporting these joint ventures already exists in the form of the Defense Enterprise Fund. The virtue of the Fund is that it is an independent, business-oriented organization dedicated to converting the Russian defense sector. In contrast to government bureaucracy, the Fund is operated by financial experts who understand markets, business plans, and investment. And in contrast to the EU's TACIS program, the Fund does not itself take on the especially demanding task of locating and identifying potential projects. Instead, it relies on entrepreneurial Russian managers and interested Western companies to locate one another, develop concrete business proposals, and then come to it for support. The job of the Fund's board of directors is to select those projects that will best support its aims of restructuring and conversion and provide them with seed capital, either in the form of equity investments or loans. The Fund is geared to absorb all profits and losses from its equity investments, with the expectation that it will be able to support itself financially in the long run.[40] At the very least, its investment income should help cover its operating costs.

The Defense Enterprise Fund may require some changes in order to enhance its effectiveness. First, the scope of its interests should be expanded beyond enterprises associated with weapons of mass destruction to encompass all types of defense outfits. Second, in coordination with other aid agencies the Fund should concentrate its efforts on enterprises in a few select, reform-oriented regions. Third, because it is an independent body, the Fund could be expanded to take in capital from the European states and Japan while including businesses from those states in its pool of potential partners for Russian firms. Although there are obvious political obstacles to such integration, arguably it would result in more effective conversion by increasing the competition among Western and Japanese companies to find and develop the best projects. Finally, to the extent that it is practicable, the Fund should emphasize projects that will benefit Russians both in terms of generating jobs and providing products that are in demand domestically.

If the commitment of the Western partners to reform in Russia proves to be a concern, another alternative would be to impose a set of requirements on them. For example, a National Academy of Sciences proposal for a joint venture mechanism suggests that the American partners sign a five-year technical and management assistance agreement for installation, training, production, product improvement, quality, marketing, sales, distribution, accounting, and finance. The goal would not only be to facilitate the operation of new production lines but also to improve the management of the entity as a business venture.[41]

The success of the Fund will depend upon adequate funding to get a first round of projects off the ground. As noted previously, the initial U.S. government capitalization has been modest: $27 million. In order to have a maximum impact through demonstrated success stories, the Fund should be given the financing it needs to do its job. It remains to be seen whether Congress and the Clinton administration will meet this challenge.

DIRECT ASSISTANCE

Although industry-industry partnership should be the centerpiece of U.S.-Russian efforts at conversion, there are a number of areas where direct assistance by Washington would be extremely valuable to Russian defense conversion, market reform, and democratization. One would be technical assistance to regional and local governments. Under the Soviet system these institutions had a very modest role in governing and delivering services to the local population. As enterprises have begun to surrender their responsibilities for apartments and social support of their workers, local governments have found themselves thrust without adequate preparation into the new role of provider and representative for their local populations. In addition to advice on service delivery, they would also benefit from Western assistance in such basic areas as financing and budgeting, how to tax effectively, and how to foster local industry and commerces.

CHAPTER 6

CONCLUSIONS

A lthough the record of success of converting and restructuring the Russian defense industries to date is mixed, there are grounds for optimism. Most important, conversion appears to be one area where assistance from the United States can make a great deal of difference in the success or failure of a Russian reform initiative. By enlisting American private industry in the creation of business partnerships with spin-offs from Russian defense enterprises, the U.S. government is using a remarkably cost-effective means of providing the Russian defense sector with many of the resources and incentives it needs to transform itself.

U.S.-Russian private joint ventures can offer targeted investment for conversion in sums far greater than Washington could provide on its own. Moreover, the profit motive drives American and Russian businesspeople to work for the project's success on its own terms and over the long run. Teaming American businesspeople with new Russian firms is also one of the most effective means of transferring the values and skills of entrepreneurship to a new generation of Russian managers and workers. Similarly, the American business partners would presumably help Russian managers organize their new firms in order to make them competitive in market conditions.

U.S. private industry benefits from such a program by gaining long-desired access to Russian industry and markets at reduced risk. The prospect of a revived Russia promises an immense consumer and capital goods market. American businesses generally see a great deal of potential in Russian defense industries. The Russian defense sector offers considerable technological and basic research capabilities, as well as well-educated, low-wage labor. One of the main obstacles for potential investors has been fear of instability. Seed capital and insurance from the U.S. government should provide the spur that many of these investors need to enter the market.

The U.S. government would benefit directly by reducing Russia's capacity to raise a military threat or contribute to proliferation of weapons around the globe. Successful conversion and restructuring of the Russian defense sector would remove a formidable political constituency for high levels of arms production and exports. Defense industry conversion will probably be necessary to the ultimate success of Russian economic reform and, perhaps, democratization. By assisting this process, therefore, the United States will be helping to forge a more durable U.S.-Russian partnership, heralding a new era of relative stability in world affairs.

Washington has already taken a number of meaningful strides toward making such programs a reality. The Nunn-Lugar Program for Cooperative Threat Reduction and its Defense Enterprise Fund provide a framework for creating conversion partnerships on a broad scale. Today, it is just a question of whether there will be sufficient political support in Congress to fund these programs sufficiently for them to have a meaningful impact. Although in the end the Defense Enterprise Fund is particularly likely to develop into a mechanism that can support itself, it nonetheless will require a firm political and financial commitment to get the process under way.

Assistance by the U.S. government and the participation of private industry, however, will not be enough to carry out successful reform of the Russian defense sector. Political and structural obstacles loom in Russia, and therefore the Russian Federation government must be an enthusiastic partner in the process. Most important, Moscow must pursue conservative monetary and fiscal policies. Without reforms to promote stability in the macroeconomy, new Russian firms will not be able to stand alone.

The Russian government must also concede that it cannot—and should not—save many existing defense enterprises. These organizations were developed for a specific purpose and according to a unique logic that no longer have any relevance. Moscow must create the policy and legal conditions in which these enterprises will turn over their assets to more efficient and marketable uses. In particular, the Russian government must implement a thoroughgoing privatization of those defense enterprises that it does not deem critical for national security. In doing so, it should permit and encourage the spinning off of departments and operations within existing enterprises in order to create new, market-worthy firms.

The Russian government will encounter substantial opposition to these policies from the current corps of managers of defense enterprises and their political allies. Indeed, having taken advantage of the reform process to reinforce themselves, many of these managers are formidable adversaries. And as long as they are confident that they will receive subsidies from the state, they will continue to resist reform. Yet beneath this management stratum, there is a great deal of dynamism in Russian enterprises and the economy generally. The task at hand, therefore, is to help those dynamic and entrepreneurial elements of the Russian economy break out and create new firms focused on competition and growth. A program of partnerships with the U.S. government and American businesses for defense conversion will be invaluable to the Russian government in its pursuit of the vast goal of transforming the legacy of the command system into an array of firms and financial institutions able to stand their ground in the global marketplace.

NOTES

INTRODUCTION

1. An analysis of the author's database of Russian enterprises reveals that over the August 1991–June 1995 period among 112 enterprises for which managerial information was available, only 21 enterprises (19 percent) experienced a change in directors. The database is the product of a review of the Soviet and Russian press during this period and enterprise information generously provided by Clifford Gaddy, Andrew Aldrin, Melanie Allen, Peter Almquist, and the U.S. Department of Commerce.

2. For example, the draft federal budget for 1995 projected a deficit equal to 30.5 percent of Russian government expenditures and 7.7 percent of gross domestic product. See Thomas Sigel, "Draft Budget Remains Unchanged Despite Chechen Crisis," *OMRI Daily Digest*, Open Media Research Institute, Prague, January 11, 1995; and Thomas Sigel, "Duma Rejects Second Reading of 1995 Draft Budget," *OMRI Daily Digest*, Open Media Research Institute, Prague, January 23, 1995.

3. One example of "off-budget financing" is provided by a reported 1995 move by President Boris Yeltsin's administration to create a special mechanism under presidential control that would export Russian oil and transfer the proceeds to defense industries. See Chrystia Freeland, "Yeltsin 'Involved in Setting Up Oil Exporter,'" *Financial Times*, January 30, 1995, p. 3.

4. The notion of enterprise *structure* used here is based on the definition used by Simon Johnson, Heidi Kroll, and Santiago Eder in "Strategy, Structure, and Spontaneous Privatization in Russia and Ukraine," in Vedat Milor, ed., *Changing Political Economies: Privatization in Post-Communist and Reforming Communist States* (Boulder, Colo.: Lynne Rienner Publishers, 1993), p. 148.

CHAPTER 1

1. This appears to be the definition used by, for example, Ann Markusen and Joel Yudken in *Dismantling the Cold War Economy* (New York: Basic Books, 1992); Thierry Malleret, *Conversion of the Defense Industry in the Former*

Soviet Union (New York: Institute for East-West Security Studies, 1992), p. 1; and the *Law on Conversion of the Defense Industry of the Russian Federation*, no. 2551–1, signed by President Boris Yeltsin, March 20, 1992, reprinted in *Rossiyskaya Gazeta* (Moscow), April 27, 1992, p. 6.

2. See Jacques S. Gansler, "Constructively Transforming the Russian Defense Industry," unpublished paper, February 28, 1994, p. 9.

3. Arthur Alexander reports that over a five-year period, only 1 percent of the establishments of multiplant firms in the United States shifted their primary output to a new product line classified in a different industry. See Arthur J. Alexander, "Perspectives on Russian Defense Industry Conversion," *Business in the Contemporary World* 5, no. 4 (Autumn 1993): 66; and Steven Lustgarten and Stavros Thomadakis, "Firm Size and Resource Mobility," final report on Contract SBA 7153-OA-83, Center for the Study of Business and Government, City University of New York, 1983, Chapter 6, cited in Alexander, note 7.

4. Gansler, "Constructively Transforming the Russian Defense Industry," p. 9. See also John Lynch, "Introduction," Robert DeGrasse, Jr., "Corporate Diversification and Conversion Experience," and Gordon Adams, "Conversion: A Dead-End Strategy?" all in John E. Lynch, ed., *Economic Adjustment and Conversion of Defense Industries* (Boulder, Colo.: Westview Press, 1987).

5. See U.S. Department of Defense, *Adjusting to the Drawdown*, report of the Defense Conversion Commission, December 31, 1992, p. 19.

6. On differences between civil and military production, see, for example, U.S. Congress, Office of Technology Assessment, *Assessing the Potential for Civil-Military Integration: Technologies, Processes, and Practices*, OTA-ISS-611, September 1994, pp. 45–47. For Russian perspectives on the problem of designing products for affordability, see the comments of V. Avduyevskiy in B. Konovalov, "Porazheniye militarizovannoy ekonomiki" (The Defeat of the Militarized Economy), *Izvestiya* (Moscow), February 7, 1990, p. 2; and aircraft designer G. V. Novozhilov, "Vystupleniya na vtorom s"ezde narodnykh deputatov SSSR (Appearances at the Second Congress of USSR People's Deputies), *Pravda* (Moscow), December 14, 1989, p. 4.

7. These definitions are based on those used by Robert M. Wallet in *Realizing the Peace Dividend: A Systems Perspective on Defense Conversion* (Washington, D.C.: Industrial College of the Armed Forces, National Defense University, 1993), pp. 3–4.

8. See David Bernstein, "Conversion," in Michael McFaul, ed., *Can the Russian Military-Industrial Complex Be Privatized? Evaluating the Experiment in Employee Ownership at the Saratov Aviation Plant*, (Stanford, Calif.: Center for International Security and Arms Control, 1993), p. 7; and Alexander, "Perspectives on Russian Defense Industry Conversion," p. 64.

9. On the strategies of U.S. defense industry firms in coping with restructuring, see Richard A. Bitzinger, "Customize Defense Industry Restructuring,"

Orbis 38, no. 2 (Spring 1994): 261–76; and Kevin P. O'Prey, *The Arms Export Challenge: Cooperative Approaches to Export Management and Defense Conversion* (Washington, D.C.: Brookings Institution, 1995), pp. 19–27.

10. Because the Soviet pricing system was more of an accounting system than a mechanism for determining the real value of goods and services, it is difficult to determine just how large the Soviet defense industries were in terms of a precise dollar or ruble figure. Rather than weigh in to a debate that will probably never be resolved, I eschew ruble and dollar figures for the Soviet economy and defense spending. The point to emphasize is that the relative militarization of the Soviet economy was much greater than that of the West. For a sample of the U.S. debates on Soviet military spending, see the summary, "Workshop I: The Size of the Military-Industrial Sector," in Michael Alexeev and Lee Walker, eds., *Estimating the Size of the Soviet Economy: Summary of a Meeting* (Washington, D.C.: National Academy Press, 1991), pp. 13–15. For an excellent analysis of the Soviet defense budgets during the perestroika period, see John Tedstrom, "*Glasnost* and the Soviet Defense Budget," *RFE/RL Report on the USSR* 4, no. 29 (July 19, 1991): 6–14. For discussion of how Soviet budget values were "established," rather than determined by markets, see D. Derek Swain, "The Soviet Military Sector: How It Is Defined and Measured," in Henry S. Rowen and Charles Wolf, Jr., eds., *The Impoverished Superpower: Perestroika and the Soviet Military Burden* (San Francisco: Institute for Contemporary Studies Press, 1990), pp. 101–2; D. Derek Swain, "Economic Constraints in Soviet Military Decision-Making," in Rowen and Wolf, *Impoverished Superpower*, pp. 206–8; and for an example of how difficult it is to determine the real costs of weapons production in the Soviet system, see the discussion of a Yakovlev aircraft designer who described the three different price accounting systems used in the Yak-42 aircraft in O. Shommer report, Vremya newscast, November 22, 1988, translated in Foreign Broadcast Information Service—Soviet Union Affairs 88–235, p. 100.

11. Cited in U.S. Department of Defense, *Soviet Military Power, 1990* (Washington, D.C.: U.S. Government Printing Office, 1990), p. 34.

12. See, for example, Julian Cooper, "Transformation of the Russian Defence Industry," *Jane's Intelligence Review*, October 1994, p. 445.

13. See Central Intelligence Agency, Directorate of Intelligence, *The Defense Industries of the Newly Independent States of Eurasia*, OSE 93–10001, January 1993, p. 5.

14. The estimate of 9 million is offered by Julian Cooper while First Deputy Minister of Defense Andrey Kokoshin estimates defense jobs as ranging between 12 and 14 million. See Julian Cooper, "The Soviet Defence Industry Heritage and Economic Restructuring in Russia," in Lars B. Wallin, ed., *The Post-Soviet Military-Industrial Complex* (Stockholm: Swedish Nations Defence Research Establishment, 1994), p. 30, drawing on the FOA

Symposium, Stockholm, October 20, 1993; and Andrey Kokoshin, "Defense Industry Conversion in the Russian Federation," in Teresa Pelton Johnson and Steven E. Miller, eds., *Russian Security after the Cold War: Seven Views from Moscow* (McLean, Va.: Brassey's, 1994), p. 48.

15. U.S. Department of Defense, *Adjusting to the Drawdown*, pp. 17–18.

16. See Kokoshin, "Defense Industry Conversion in the Russian Federation," p. 48.

17. See Table 2–3 in Logistics Management Institute, *Impacts of Defense Spending Cuts on Industry Sectors, Occupational Groups, and Localities*, Bethesda, Md., February 1993, Annex F of U.S. Department of Defense, *Adjusting to the Drawdown*. Note that the figure for electronics production in the United States refers to *employment* while the Soviet figures refer to *output*. A comparison between the two measures is nonetheless possible.

18. For example, during the Brezhnev years investment accounted for about 30 percent of Soviet gross national product while nonfood consumer goods production averaged between 8 and 10 percent of GNP. Even in that welfare state writ large, services only accounted on average during this period for 18–19 percent of GNP. See U.S. Congress, Joint Economic Committee, "USSR: Shares of GNP by End Use," S.Prt. 101–123, 102d Cong., 2d sess., November 1990, Table 1–10, p. 82.

19. See David F. Epstein, "The Economic Cost of Soviet Security and Empire," in Rowen and Wolf, *Impoverished Superpower*, pp. 143–46; and Shelley Deutch, "The Soviet Weapons Industry: An Overview," in *Gorbachev's Economic Plans* (Washington, D.C.: U.S. Government Printing Office, 1987), vol. 1, p. 407. On the causes and effects of shortage in Soviet-type economies, see, for example, Alec Nove, *The Soviet Economic System*, 2d ed. (London: Allen & Unwin, 1980).

20. See Christopher M. Davis, "The High Priority Sector in a Shortage Economy," in Rowen and Wolf, *Impoverished Superpower*, pp. 171–72; and David F. Epstein, "The Economic Cost of Soviet Security and Empire," in Rowen and Wolf, *Impoverished Superpower*, p. 145. According to economist Yevgeniy Kuznetsov, there were probably substantial differences in wages among the nine sectors of the defense industries, with high-technology sectors like aviation building offering higher wages than lower-tech sectors such as tank production. Personal communication between Kuznetsov and the author.

21. Epstein, "Economic Cost of Soviet Security and Empire," pp. 143–46.

22. See Gertrude Schroeder, *The System Versus Progress: Soviet Economic Problems* (London: Centre for Research into Communist Economies, 1986), p. 18.

23. See Peter Almquist, "Soviet Military Acquisition: From a Seller's Market to a Buyer's?" in Susan L. Clark, ed., *Soviet Military Power in a Changing World* (Boulder, Colo.: Westview Press, 1991), p. 143; Matthew Partan, "Who Controlled the Former-Soviet Military Industry?" *Soviet Defense Notes* (MIT Post-Soviet Security Studies Working Group) 4, no. 1 (March 1992); and author

interviews with a Soviet General Staff official, Cambridge, Mass., September 1992, and with defense enterprise directors, Moscow, April 1994.

24. Belousov was citing with approval a statement made by his personal mentor. Arthur J. Alexander, "Interviews with Soviet Military Industrial Complex Leaders: VPK Chairman Belousov and Central Committee Secretary Baklanov," unpublished report, December 1990.

25. See, for example, Paul L. Joskow, Richard Schmalensee, and Natalia Tsukanova, "Competition Policy in Russia during and after Privatization," *Brookings Papers on Economic Activity: Microeconomics 1994*, Brookings Institution, Washington, D.C., 1994, pp. 307–9, 311; and Peter Almquist, *Red Forge: Soviet Military Industry since 1965* (New York: Columbia University Press, 1990).

26. Alexander Ozhegov, for example, cites the practically nonexistent interaction between the fourteen defense enterprises in the republic of Udmurtiya, which were divided between eight different branch ministries. See Alexander Ozhegov, "Conversion and Russia's Regions," in Wallin, *Post-Soviet Military-Industrial Complex*, p. 59.

27. See, for example, Ed A. Hewett, *Reforming the Soviet Economy: Equality versus Efficiency* (Washington, D.C.: Brookings Institution, 1988), pp. 171–74.

28. See Annette N. Brown, Barry W. Ickes, and Randi Ryterman, "The Myth of Monopoly: A New View of Industrial Structure in Russia," World Bank Policy Research Working Paper no. 1331, Washington, D.C., August 1994, pp. 30–32.

29. Many defense industrial ministries reconstituted themselves to become large holding companies, concerns, and other types of commercial organizations. However, lacking their former role as state institutions and possessing very little in the way of investment resources, these organizations appear to be largely irrelevant.

30. Schroeder, *System Versus Progress*, p. 86. Throughout this paper, therefore, a distinction is drawn between enterprises and firms.

31. Joskow, Schmalensee, and Tsukanova, "Competition Policy in Russia," pp. 312–15.

32. See Clifford G. Gaddy, *Civilianizing Russia: How Factories and Families Are Adjusting to Life in a Non-militarized Economy* (Washington, D.C.: Brookings Institution, forthcoming).

33. Znamya Truda—also known as Demen'tyev Aviation Production Association—has since become the main component of the Moscow Aviation Production Association (MAPO). U.S. Department of Commerce, *Russian Defense Business Directory: 1993* (Washington, D.C.: U.S. Government Printing Office, 1993), pp. 36, 38.

34. There are a large number of American *firms* with workforces reckoned in the tens of thousands. But, as noted above, these employees are spread across numerous different establishments and geographically distinct facilities within the firm. See Joskow, Schmalensee, and Tsukanova, "Competition Policy in Russia," p. 312.

The definition of "establishment" used here is derived from the Standard Industrial Code (SIC) Manual: "an economic unit, generally at a single location, where . . . industrial operations are performed. (For example: a factory, mill, . . ." See U.S. Office of Management and Budget, *Standard Industrial Classification Manual—1987* (Springfield, Va.: National Technical Information Service, 1987), p. 12.

35. Joskow, Schmalensee, and Tsukanova, "Competition Policy in Russia," p. 313; and Brown, Ickes, and Ryterman, "Myth of Monopoly," pp. 15–17.

36. Center of the Economic Analysis and Forecasts, *Rossiya—1993: Ekonomicheskaya Kon"yunktura* (Russia—1993: Economic Performance), Moscow, February 1993, Table VI.5, p. 157.

37. See David Bernstein, "Spin-offs and Start-ups in Russia: A Key Element of Industrial Restructuring," in Michael McFaul and Tova Perlmutter, eds., *Privatization, Conversion, and Enterprise Reform in Russia* (Stanford, Calif.: Center for International Security and Arms Control, May 1994), pp. 201–15.

38. According to economist Ed Hewett, for example, by the 1980s most new enterprises were being designed to be as self-sufficient as possible. See Hewett, *Reforming the Soviet Economy*, p. 173.

39. See Nikolay Belan, "Izhevskiy oruzheyniki" (The Izhevsk Gunsmiths), *Krasnaya Zvezda* (Moscow), September 9, 1992, pp. 1, 4.

40. See Yelena Druzhinina, "The Defense Industry Is Revealing Its Cards," *Delovoy Mir*, November 2, 1991, p. 8, translated in Joint Publications Research Service—Soviet Union Military Affairs 91-031, pp. 62–64.

41 See Aleksey Shulunov, "K chemu vedyet byudzhetnaya strategiya pravitel'stva" (To What the Government's Budgetary Strategy Is Leading), *Nezavisimaya Gazeta* (Moscow), June 8, 1994, pp. 1–2.

42. Ksenya Gonchar, senior researcher at the Institute of World Economy and International Relations (IMEMO) of the Russian Academy of Sciences, "Employment Aspects of Defense Conversion in Russia," mimeo, May 1994, footnote 13.

43. See Markusen and Yudken, *Dismantling the Cold War Economy*, pp. 170–207.

44. Stepan Sulakshin, "Dva kvartala na golodnom paykye" (Two-quarters' Starvation Rations), *Krasnaya Zvezda* (Moscow), May 28, 1994, p. 3.

45. Among these were Chelyabinsk-40, Chelyabinsk-65, Chelyabinsk-70, Arzamas-16, Krasnoyarsk-45, Krasnoyarsk-26, and Tomsk-7. See Julian Cooper, *The Soviet Defence Industry: Conversion and Economic Reform* (New York: Council on Foreign Relations Press, 1991), pp. 25–26. For an analysis of recent developments in Arzamas-16, see Kimberly Marten-Zisk, "Arzamas-16: Economics and Security in a Closed Nuclear City," *Post-Soviet Affairs* 11, no. 1 (January–March 1995): 57–80.

46. Logistics Management Institute, *Impacts of Defense Spending Cuts*, Table 3–2. Note that there is a difference in definition for the two categories of workers described here. "Industrial" in the Russian case includes only jobs in manufacturing and mining, while the U.S. employment figures

concern nonfarm, private-sector employment. The categories are comparable for illustrative purposes if only because historically the service sector in the USSR/Russia has been very small.

47. In a case study of a defense-dependent city conducted by the author, the growth of the long-neglected service sector was helping to soak up many of the workers leaving local defense plants. See the discussion in the "Government Strategy Has Been Faulty" section of Chapter 3 of this paper. For discussion of other defense-dependent cities, see Clair K. Blong and James R. Lecky, "Converting Defense Industry in Nizhniy Novgorod: A Preliminary Analysis," National Defense University, Washington, D.C., November 1993; and Clair K. Blong and James R. Lecky, "Converting Russian Defense Industry: A Preliminary Analysis of Kaluga Oblast," National Defense University, Washington, D.C., July 26, 1994.

48. See Kokoshin, "Defense Industry Conversion in the Russian Federation," p. 25.

49. Cooper cites former prime minister Nikolay Ryzhkov. See Cooper, *Soviet Defence Industry*, p. 14.

50. Yevgeniy Kuznetsov, "Downsizing the Defense Industry in the Former Soviet Union: Implications for the United States," in Ethan B. Kapstein, ed., *Downsizing Defense* (Washington, D.C.: Congressional Quarterly Press, 1993), p. 172; and Cooper, "Soviet Defence Industry Heritage," p. 33.

51. Vitaliy Shlykov, "The Defense Industry and Democracy in Russia: The Interplay," mimeo, Fall 1993; and Epstein, "Economic Cost of Soviet Security and Empire," pp. 135–36.

52. See, for example, the discussion in Epstein, "Economic Cost of Soviet Security and Empire," pp. 141–42; and Ozhegov, "Conversion and Russia's Regions," p. 53.

53. See Yevgeniy Kuznetsov, "Adjustment of the Russian Defence-Related Enterprises: Macroeconomic Implications," mimeo, Institute for Economic Forecasting, Moscow, October 1993, pp. 8–9. According to David Bernstein and Elaine Naugle, the director of the new high-tech firm ELVIS+ believes that there is no acceptable electronics production capability in the former Soviet Union. Thus, the director prefers offshore production for his electronics needs. See David Bernstein and Elaine Naugle, "ELVIS+ and the Moscow Center for SPARC Technology (MCST)," in David Bernstein, ed., *Defense Industry Restructuring in Russia: Case Studies and Analysis* (Stanford, Calif.: Center for International Security and Arms Control, December 1994), p. 36.

54. Kuznetsov, "Adjustment of the Russian Defence-Related Enterprises," p. 8.

55. Ibid., pp. 8–9.

CHAPTER 2

1. On the history of the perestroika reforms, see Anders Åslund, *Gorbachev's Struggle for Economic Reform* (Ithaca, N.Y.: Cornell University Press, 1991).

2. Julian Cooper, *The Soviet Defence Industry: Conversion and Economic Reform* (New York: Council on Foreign Relations Press, 1991), p. 31.

3. The Ministry of Light and Food Industry was formally disbanded on March 1, 1988. Evidently, in addition to the transfer of jurisdiction over enterprises, the government also assigned a number of agricultural/industrial product orders to the defense sector. See Arthur Alexander, "The Conversion of Soviet Defense Industry," RAND Paper P-7620, RAND Corporation, Santa Monica, Calif., January 1990, pp. 11–13.

4. See Vitaliy Portnykov, "M. Gorbachev: This Is Our Last-Ditch Attempt," *Molod Ukrayniy*, December 1, 1990, translated in Foreign Broadcast Information Service—Soviet Union Affairs (hereafter, FBIS-SOV) 90-082, pp. 84–85.

5. On the decisionmaking process and its participants, see Kevin P. O'Prey, "The Brave New World of the Soviet Defense Sector," *Breakthroughs* (a publication of the MIT Defense and Arms Control Studies Program) 1, no. 2 (Spring 1991): 6.

6. Georgiy Dolzhenko, "We Shall Beat Our Swords into Potato Peelers: Substituting the Economic Levers of Conversion for 'Willful' Directives Is Absurd," *Rabochaya Tribuna* (Moscow), May 25, 1991, p. 2, translated in Joint Publications Research Service—Soviet Union Economic Affairs (hereafter, JPRS-UEA) 91-028, pp. 4–106.

The general designer of Sukhoy fighter aircraft complained similarly that he was assigned the task of developing packing machines for bulk products. See the comments of M. P. Simonov in Dmitriy Khrapovitskiy, *Soyuz*, no. 7 (February 12–18, 1990): 14, translated in Joint Publications Research Service—Soviet Union Military Affairs (hereafter, JPRS-UMA) 90-014, pp. 84–87.

7. According to the bitter general director of NPO Saturn, "We had to engage in the development and improvement of machines for the leather and fur industry: beginning with the skinning of the animal and ending with the dressing and dyeing of the hide." See Colonel A. Manushkin, "Turbiny, luk, ovech'i shkury . . . i takoye sochetaniye byvaet, esli v konversiyu vtorgaetsya volyutarizm" (Turbines, Onions, and Sheepskins . . . There Will Be such a Combination if Voluntarism Meddles with Conversion), *Krasnaya Zvezda* (Moscow), February 12, 1991, p. 2.

8. S. Mikheyev, "Konversiy mozhet dat' obshchestvu miliardy dolarov esli vybrat' vernyy kurs" (Conversion Can Provide Billions of Dollars to Society if the Right Course Is Chosen), *Izvestiya* (Moscow), March 23, 1990, p. 2.

9. As cited in an interview with A. Pokrovskiy, "Vsyo nachinaetsya s cheloveka" (Everything Starts from Man), *Pravda* (Moscow), December 9, 1989, p. 3.

10. On the 1987 Law on the State Enterprise, see Gertrude E. Schroeder, "Anatomy of Gorbachev's Economic Reform," in Ed A. Hewett and Victor H. Winston, eds., *Milestones in Glasnost and Perestroyka: The Economy* (Washington, D.C.: Brookings Institution, 1991), pp. 206–8.

Later, during the so-called war of laws between the center and the republics, the Russian Federation enacted the 1990 Law on Enterprises and Entrepreneurial Activity. Although its legal status was contested, the law mandated that the directors of Russian enterprises would be elected by the *owners* of their enterprise. See Simon Johnson and Heidi Kroll, "Managerial Strategies for Spontaneous Privatization," *Soviet Economy* 7, no. 4 (October–December 1991): 287.

11. Kornai argues, "Although there is a budget constraint that forces some financial discipline upon the firm, it is not strictly binding, but can be 'stretched' at the will of the higher authorities. In principle, the firm should cover expenditures from revenues made on the market. In practice, earnings from the market can be arbitrarily supplemented by external assistance." See Janos Kornai, "The Hungarian Reform Process: Visions, Hopes, and Reality," *Journal of Economic Literature* 24, no. 4 (December 1986): 1697–98.

12. Johnson and Kroll, "Managerial Strategies for Spontaneous Privatization," p. 287.

13. Andrey Kokoshin, "Defense Industry Conversion in the Russian Federation," in Teresa Pelton Johnson and Steven E. Miller, eds., *Russian Security after the Cold War: Seven Views from Moscow* (McLean, Va.: Brassey's, 1994), p. 58.

14. Julian Cooper argues that between 1989 and 1990 the Soviet government implemented a 30 percent cut in arms procurement. Alexander Ozhegov asserts that a 30 percent annual drop in defense production continued until 1992. See Julian Cooper, "The Soviet Defence Industry Heritage and Economic Restructuring in Russia," in Lars B. Wallin, ed., *The Post-Soviet Military-Industrial Complex* (Stockholm: Swedish Nations Defence Research Establishment, 1994), p. 36, drawing on the FOA Symposium, Stockholm, October 20, 1993; and Alexander Ozhegov, "Conversion and Russia's Regions," in Wallin, *Post-Soviet Military-Industrial Complex*, p. 53.

15. According to Alexander Ozhegov, the costs of maintaining these reserves were very high, leading to price increases for the remaining civil and military production. In some cases, the overhead costs of maintaining these idle capacities was 700–800 percent. See Ozhegov, "Conversion and Russia's Regions," p. 53.

16. By 1990, the defense sector had actually started production of only 23 out of 120 types of new products that had been assigned to it. Of these 23 "successes," only 5 met international quality standards. Reportedly, the results for 1991 were even worse. See S. Leskov, "Pokhozhe, voyennaya promyshlennost' gotovit revansh" (It Seems that the Military Industry Is Preparing Its Revenge), *Izvestiya* (Moscow), December 5, 1991, p. 2.

17. Yevgeniy Panov and Aleksandr Osipov, "Conversion—From the Zone of Militarism to the Free Zone," *Rossiyskaya Gazeta* (Moscow), Sept 12, 1991, p. 2, translated in JPRS-UMA 91-027, pp. 39–44.

18. Leskov, "Pokhozhe, voyennaya promyshlennost' gotovit revansh"; and D. Bikov, "Swords into Plowshares: How the Defense Branches Are Making the Transition to Peaceful Production," *Selskaya Zhizn'* (Moscow), August 1, 1989, p. 2, translated in FBIS-SOV 89-155, pp. 115–17.

19. See Peter Almquist and Kevin O'Prey, "Beating Swords into Agricultural Complexes: Soviet Economic Conversion," *Arms Control Today*, December 1990, p. 19.

20. Sevmash was actually able to sell several of these submarines to tour operators in the Caribbean, who painted them yellow. See Andrey Naryshkin, "Gde rozhdayutsya submariny" (Where the Submarines Are Produced), *Rossiyskiye Vesti* (Moscow), November 20, 1992, p. 3. But consider that the plant had the capacity to build ten or twenty large, highly complex military submarines each year and the waste of production resources becomes apparent.

21. Alexander, "Conversion of Soviet Defense Industry," pp. 9–10.

22. By the time of the coup, GDP was predicted to be heading for an 18 percent decline for 1991. See Peter Murrell, "What is Shock Therapy? What Did It Do in Poland and Russia?" *Post-Soviet Affairs* 9, no. 2 (April–June 1993): 132.

23. See Simon Johnson, Heidi Kroll, and Santiago Eder, "Strategy, Structure, and Spontaneous Privatization in Russia and Ukraine," in Vedat Milor, ed., *Changing Political Economies: Privatization in Post-Communist and Reforming Communist States* (Boulder, Colo.: Lynne Rienner Publishers, 1993), p. 157; and Donna Bahry, "The Union Republics and Contradictions in Gorbachev's Economic Reform," *Soviet Economy* 7, no. 3 (July–September 1991): 216, 245–47.

24. The chief of the Soviet general staff, General Mikhail Moiseyev, complained in February 1990 that the cost to the Ministry of Defense of some types of equipment and services had increased 200–300 percent. See Viktor Litovkin, "Argumenty general'nogo shtaba" (Arguments of the General Staff), *Izvestiya* (Moscow), February 22, 1990, p. 3. Regarding the problem of enterprise managers ignoring orders, one defense manager complained in 1990 that he had received an ultimatum from one of his suppliers: "If you want to receive components, you must dispatch us cars and lumber." See Y. Sharipov, "Swords into Washtubs," *Sovetskaya Rossiya*, February 24, 1990, p. 1, translated in JPRS-UMA, June 26, 1990, pp. 45–46.

25. On the problems of opting for self-financing and autonomy before price liberalization, see the comments of Ed Hewett in Abel Aganbegyan et al., "Basic Directions of Perestroyka," in Hewett and Winston, *Milestones in Glasnost and Perestroyka*, pp. 111–12. See also Schroeder, "Anatomy of Gorbachev's Economic Reform," pp. 217–23.

26. Johnson, Kroll, and Eder, "Strategy, Structure, and Spontaneous Privatization in Russia and Ukraine," p. 286.

27. Formerly the economics editor of the liberal Communist Party journal *Kommunist*, Gaydar joined the Russian government as deputy prime

minister and minister of the economy and finance in November 1991. In April 1992, he became acting prime minister. See Anders Åslund, *How Russia Became a Market Economy* (Washington, D.C.: Brookings Institution, 1995).

28. Most of the *devyatka* were reorganized as departments under the Ministry of Industry, which itself was later downgraded to a state committee. The only exception was the nuclear weapons and energy sector, which continued to have its own branch ministry.

29. Research and development orders were pared at a much lesser rate. Defense R&D was cut by 18 percent while civil R&D was reduced by 38 percent. See Cooper, "The Soviet Defence Industry Heritage," p. 36. In a fall 1991 article, Gaydar explained the rationale for the defense sector was "to maintain the wage costs, social programs, and part of the allocations to military research, *but to cut arms procurement with the utmost severity.*" (author's emphasis) See Yegor Gaydar, "The Race with the Crisis," *Novoye Vremya*, no. 48 (1991): 13, as cited in Åslund, *How Russia Became a Market Economy*, p. 66.

30. Article 4 of the Russian Federation's Law on Conversion specifies: "The main role in organizing the switch from military to civil production and the drawing up of conversion programs *belongs to the defense enterprise.*" (author's emphasis) See *Russian Federation Law on Conversion of the Defense Industry in the Russian Federation*, no. 2551-1, March 20, 1992, reprinted in translation in FBIS-SOV 92-083, pp. 27–30. According to the assistant to then deputy prime minister Georgiy Khizha, Andrei Gorbachev, the Federation government also began transferring responsibility for the maintenance and development of defense enterprises to the regional level. See Andrei O. Gorbachev, "Defense Conversion: Problems and Solutions," in Michael P. Claudon and Kathryn Wittneben, eds., *After the Cold War: Russian-American Defense Conversion for Economic Renewal* (New York: New York University Press, 1993), p. 37.

31. See Andrei Kuznetsov, "Economic Reforms in Russia: Enterprise Behaviour as an Impediment to Change," *Europe-Asia Studies* (Glasgow) 46, no. 6 (1994): 955–58. In August Gaydar complained bitterly about vested interests: "The military industrial complex, the agrarian lobby, and associations of sectors demanding subsidies and customs protection are putting too much effort, money and time into safeguarding their share of the taxpayers' money for them to be driven away all that simply from the state pie." See Yegor Gaydar, "Rossiya i Reformy" (Russia and Reforms), *Izvestiya* (Moscow), August 19, 1992, p. 2.

32. Surprisingly, only one of the three proved to be conservative once in the government. Shumeyko sympathized with the reformers from the start while Chernomyrdin ultimately joined them in practice, if not in spirit. See Åslund, *How Russia Became a Market Economy*, p. 95.

33. These conservatives included Yuriy Skokov and Oleg Lobov, both of whom had roles on the Security Council. Other pro-defense industry figures in the government included the presidential adviser on conversion, Mikhail Maley, the chairman of the state committee for conversion, Mikhail Bazhanov, and Minister of Industry Aleksandr Titkin. Vice President Aleksandr Rutskoy was also strongly opposed to reform, but he was not particularly close to Yeltsin.

34. For a chronology of these developments, see Barry W. Ickes and Randi Ryterman, "Roadblock to Economic Reform: Inter-Enterprise Debt and the Transition to Markets," *Post-Soviet Affairs* 9, no. 3 (July–September 1993): 235–36, 238. Because most of these credits were provided at an interest rate that was less than the inflation rate, they amounted to outright grants rather than loans.

35. See Christine Williams, deputy director, Office of Slavic and Eurasian Analysis, Central Intelligence Agency, Statement for the Record to the Technology and National Security Subcommittee, U.S. Congress, Joint Economic Committee, 103d Cong., 1st sess., June 11, 1993.

36. The state privatization program approved in June 1992 classified defense enterprises in a category prohibited from privatizing without approval of the government.

37. According to Anders Åslund, Yeltsin was prepared to cave in to the demands of the defense sector, but Chernomyrdin successfully held firm. See Anders Åslund, "Russia's Success Story," *Foreign Affairs* 73, no. 5 (September/October 1994): 64.

38. Åslund, *How Russia Became a Market Economy*, pp. 187–207.

39. See Mark Nagel, "The 1994 Budget," mimeo, May 16, 1994, as cited in ibid., p. 199.

40. Author interviews with defense enterprise directors and analysts at Russian Academy of Sciences institutes, April 1994.

41. Åslund, *How Russia Became a Market Economy*, p. 199.

42. Åslund, *How Russia Became a Market Economy*, p. 203.

43. Chernomyrdin has stated publicly that the solution to the crisis in the defense sector is privatization and financial discipline on the parts of the directors. See the speech of Premier Viktor Chernomyrdin at the July 15, 1994, Russian Federation government session, "Sterzhen' raboty Pravitel'stva vo vtorom polugodii—strukturnaya perestroyka khozyaystva," (The Core of the Government's Work in the Second Half of the Year—Restructuring the Economy) *Rossiyskiye Vesti* (Moscow), July 19, 1994, pp. 1, 4.

44. Julian Cooper, "Transforming Russia's Defence Industrial Base," *Survival* 35, no. 4 (Winter 1993): 147–62; and presidential ukase no. 1267 (classified), *Ob osobennostyakh privatizatsii i dopolnitel'nykh merakh gosudarstvennogo regulirovaniya deyatel'nosti predpriyatiy oboronnykh otrasley promyshlennosti* (On the Special Features of Privatization and

Supplementary Measures of State Regulation of the Activity of Enterprises of the Defense Sectors of Industry), August 19, 1993.

45. According to Alfred Koch, the deputy chairman of the State Property Committee, by the end of 1994, 1,550 out of 2,000 defense enterprises will have been privatized. See Keith Bush, "Most Defense Enterprises to Be Privatized by End 1994," Radio Free Europe/Radio Liberty *Daily Report*, March 1, 1994.

46. A. Rodionov, deputy director of Rosoboronprom, commentary on ukase no. 1267, *Ob osobennostyakh privatizatsii*, transcribed by A. Yakovleva in "Privatizatsiya VPK uporyadochivaetsya" (The Privatization of the MIC Is Put in Order), *Ekonomika i Zhizn'* (Moscow), no. 37 (September 1993): 18.

47. For a description of the options available to privatizing defense enterprises, see Eva Busza, "Strategies of Privatization: The Options," in Michael McFaul, ed., *Can the Russian Military-Industrial Complex Be Privatized? Evaluating the Experiment in Employee Ownership at the Saratov Aviation Plant* (Stanford, Calif.: Center for International Security and Arms Control, May 1993), pp. 29–40.

48. Rodionov, "Privatizatsiya VPK uporyadochivaetsya"; and presidential ukase no. 1267.

49. See point 7 of presidential ukase no. 1267, *Ob osobennostyakh privatizatsii.*

50. See Randall Forsberg and Jonathan Cohen, "Issues and Choices in Arms Production and Trade," in Randall Forsberg, ed., *The Arms Production Dilemma: Contraction and Restraint in the World Combat Aircraft Industry* (Cambridge, Mass.: MIT Press, 1994), Table 12.1.

51. Peter Almquist, "Soviet-Russian Procurement Database," January 1995. The author would like to thank Peter Almquist for generously providing him with this source.

52. See Aleksey Shulunov, "K chemu vedyet byudzhetnaya strategiya pravitel'stva" (To What the Government's Budgetary Strategy Is Leading), *Nezavisimaya Gazeta* (Moscow), June 8, 1994, pp. 1–2.

53. See Almquist, "Soviet-Russian Procurement Database"; Marina Chernuka and Vyacheslav Terekhov, interview with First Deputy Minister of Defense Andrey Kokoshin, Interfax (Moscow), 0545 GMT, July 24, 1992, translated in FBIS-SOV 92-143, July 24, 1992; and Shulunov, "K chemu vedyet byudzhetnaya strategiya pravitel'stva."

54. See William Grundmann, director for combat support, U.S. Defense Intelligence Agency, statement for the record to the Joint Economic Committee, U.S. Congress, 103d Cong., 2d sess., July 15, 1994, Table 1.

55. See the statements of Viktor Glukhikh in Yelena Belova, "Oboronnyy zakaz v 1994 godu sokrashchen ne budet: Torgovlya noveyshim oruzhiyem vygodnee konversii, schitayut oboronshchiki" (Defense Orders Will Not Be Cut in 1994: Trade in the Most Modern Weapons Is More Profitable than Conversion, the Defense Industrialists Believe), *Segodnya* (Moscow), December 25, 1993, p. 2; and Vitaliy Y. Vitebskiy, head of the main directorate

of information and statistics of Goskomoboronprom, "VPK: Itogi 1994 goda" (The MIC: 1994 Results), mimeo, January 20, 1995. The author thanks Yevgeniy Kuznetsov for providing this document.

56. See the comments of Viktor Glukhikh in Keith Bush, "Decline of Defense Industry Decried," Radio Free Europe/Radio Liberty *Daily Report*, April 28, 1994; the decline in both civil and military production in the defense sector was, in fact, intensifying during the early months of 1995. See Vitaliy Vitebskiy, "VPK v Fevralye" (The MIC in February), *Krasnaya Zvezda* (Moscow), March 25, 1995, p. 3.

57. The exception to the rule, of course, is the *external* brain drain of nuclear weapons scientists, rocket engineers, etc. to outlaw states such as Libya, Iran, Iraq, and North Korea.

58. Oleg Antonov, "VPK Mertv: O maloizvestnykh prichinakh krizisa na predpriyatiyakh voeyenno-promyshlennogo kompleksa" (The MIC Is Dead: About Little-Known Reasons for the Crisis at Enterprises of the Military-Industrial Complex), *Nezavisimaya Gazeta* (Moscow), September 1, 1994, p. 4.

59. This particular firm—Ural ExIm—was founded in November 1991 by a former defense manager who had been able to obtain low-interest credits. Through its own financial resources and with the help of the Perm' city administration, in 1993 the firm was able to buy property on which it erected a new factory with 4,000 square meters of floor space and new equipment. Author interviews with enterprise director and city officials, Perm', April 1994.

60. One estimate argues that 1.5 million workers were laid off by the defense industries in 1993. See Inna Rozanova, "If You Have No Job You Cannot Lose It," *Rossiyskaya Gazeta* (Moscow), May 27, 1994, p. 3, translated in JPRS-UMA 94-025, pp. 42–44.

61. Anders Åslund cites Russian Government officials describing the labor force as 3 million employees. Stepan Sulakshin, the chairman of the State Duma Military-Industrial Complex Subcommittee, however, offers a higher estimate of 4.5 million workers. An unidentified official from the State Committee on the Defense Branches of Industry provides an estimate between these two: 3.6 million defense workers. Russian economist Ksenya Gonchar estimates that defense industry employment in early 1992 was 4.5 million people, declining to 3.5 million people by the beginning of 1994. Of these, Gonchar estimates, only one-third are involved in military work. See Åslund, "Russia's Success Story," p. 65; Stepan Sulakshin, "Dva kvartala na golodnom paykye" (Two-quarters' Starvation Rations), *Krasnaya Zvezda* (Moscow), May 28, 1994, p. 3; Doug Clarke, "Brain-Drain Hurts Defense Industry," Radio Free Europe/Radio Liberty *Daily Report*, November 15, 1994; and Ksenya Gonchar, senior researcher at the Institute of World Economy and International Relations (IMEMO) of the Russian Academy of Sciences, "Employment Aspects of Defense Conversion in Russia," mimeo, May 1994.

62. Gonchar also found that the extent of the brain drain is worse in the defense sector than in civilian-oriented enterprises, although the gap between them has been shrinking recently. See Gonchar, "Employment Aspects of Defense Conversion in Russia," pp. 6–7; and E. Roganov, "O rinke truda v Udmurtii," (About the Labor Market in Udmurtiya), *Chelovek i Trud*, no. 12 (1993): 31–32, cited in Gonchar, "Employment Aspects of Defense Conversion in Russia."

63. Author interviews with defense enterprise directors and city officials, Perm', April 1994.

64. Aleksandr Veklich, "Ekskavator sobran na 80 protsentov iz 'oboron-nykh' detaley" (80 Percent of the Excavator Is Assembled from 'Military Parts'), *Krasnaya Zvezda* (Moscow), December 15, 1993, p. 1.

65. Author interviews with a defense enterprise shop director as well as city and oblast officials, Perm', April 1994.

66. See German Lomanov, "VPIK Is Beginning: Who Will Gain?" *Delovoy Mir*, July 22, 1992, p. 7, translated in JPRS-UMA 92-036, pp. 54–57; and Vladimir Mikhaylov, "Za okeanom konkurenty tozhe ne trebuyutsya" (Competitors Are Also Not Required Abroad), *Rossiyskaya Gazeta* (Moscow), August 7, 1992, p. 3.

67. See Tarja Cronberg, "Enterprise Strategies to Cope with Reduced Defense Spending: The Experience of the Perm Region," in Michael McFaul and Tova Perlmutter, eds., *Privatization, Conversion, and Enterprise Reform in Russia* (Stanford, Calif.: Center for International Security and Arms Control, May 1994), p. 191.

68. In a survey of Western chief executive offices who have visited Russian plants manufactuing products similar to their own, Kathryn Wittneben found that most believed the Russian plants were poorly laid out, possessed a redundant workforce, were hampered by an inefficient manufacturing flow, and were plain unsafe. Figuring in many cases that it would take too much capital investment to fix the existing facility, they often argued for starting anew. See Kathryn Wittneben, "Perspectives and the Role of U.S. Business in Russian Defense Conversion," in Claudon and Wittneben, *After the Cold War*.

69. Il'ya Shkabara, Andrey Skvortsov, and the Merkator Group, "'Sil'nyye' regiony Rossii poluchat dopolnitel'nyye sredstva: A slbyye mogut nadeyat'sya na off-shor" (The 'Strong' Regions of Russia Will Get Additional Funds: And the Weak Ones Can Hope for the Offshore), *Segodnya* (Moscow), May 14, 1994, p. 3; and Vitaliy Vitebskiy, "VPK v Yanvarye" (The MIC in January), *Krasnaya Zvezda* (Moscow), February 25, 1995, p. 3.

70. Ozhegov, "Conversion and Russia's Regions," pp. 50–51. Members of the Russian military still complain that the electronics industry failed them during the Soviet period. One official, for example, asserted that problems with the performance and lack of miniaturization of domestic electronics forced the military to increase the size of its submarines, restrict the systems on board combat aircraft, and fly more satellites than the

West because of the limited service life. See Aleksandr Anatolyevich Ivanov and Lev Ivanovich Titov, untitled article in *Vooruzheniye, Politika, Konversiya* 4, no. 1 (August 4, 1994): 45–50, translated in JPRS-UMA 94-056, pp. 29–32.

71. See Center for Economic Conditions under the Russian Federation Government, "Defense Enterprises and Their 1994 Prospects," *Delovoy Mir,* August 27, 1994, p. 5, translated in JPRS-UMA 94-038, pp. 25–32; and Y. N. Kulichkov and V. D. Kalachapov, "Analysis of Production-Economic Activities of Enterprises of the Defense Branches of Industry under the Conditions of the Conversion of Military Production," *Voprosy Ekonomiki i Konversii,* no. 1 (1994): 3–8, translated in JPRS-UMA 94-038, pp. 22–25.

72. Author's interviews with defense enterprise directors and city officials, Perm', April 1994 and May 1995. Given the loss of work, Velta's management has taken the wise step of shedding some of its workforce.

73. The author would like to thank Clifford Gaddy for pointing out this fact.

74. See Andrey Bagrov and Andrey Sinitsyn, "The Kirov Plant Has Shut Down: The Putilov Workers Have Gone on Leave until October," *Kommersant-Daily* (Moscow), March 12, 1994, p. 3, translated in JPRS-UMA 94-026, pp. 42–43.

75. Author's database. If true, this is a remarkably low rate of managerial turnover: it would mean that the average manager remains in office for twenty years before retiring. Given the economic difficulties that have confronted defense managers since the beginning of perestroika and especially since the collapse of the Soviet Union, it is striking that many have not just opted to retire. For an account of a manager voted out of office because the workers in his enterprise had lost faith in him, see the case of NPO Impuls as described in Tova Perlmutter, Michael McFaul, and Elaine Naugle, "Impuls," in Bernstein, *Defense Industry Restructuring in Russia,* p. 46.

76. In November 1993 President Yeltsin complained that more than four hundred defense enterprises had not yet begun to implement conversion plans. See report of ITAR-TASS (in English), 1532 GMT, November 16, 1993, reprinted in FBIS-SOV 93-220, p. 60.

77. See interview (by unidentified correspondent) with A. A. Kokoshin, first deputy minister of defense of the Russian Federation, on the "Aty Baty" program, Moscow Russian Television and Dubl Networks, 2305 GMT, April 17, 1993, translated in FBIS-SOV 93-073, pp. 51–52; and A. A. Kokoshin, "Protivorechiya formirovaniya i puti razvitiya voenno-tekhnicheskoy politiki Rossiy" (Contradictions of Formation and Ways of Developing the Military-Technical Policy of Russia), *Voyennaya Mysl'* (Moscow), no. 2 (1993).

78. Kulichkov and Kalachapov, "Analysis of Production-Economic Activities of Enterprises."

79. The survey sample was 158 enterprises. See Center for Economic Conditions under the Russian Federation Government, "Defense Enterprises and Their 1994 Prospects."

80. Only 3 percent of enterprises surveyed expected an increase in their

labor force. Ibid.

81. "Another Military Installation Is Deprived of Electricity," *Segodnya* (Moscow), September 24, 1994, p. 1, translated in FBIS-SOV 94-186, p. 28.

82. Igor Khripunov, Center for East-West Trade Policy, University of Georgia, "Russia's Arms Trade in the Post Cold War Period," *Washington Quarterly* 17, no. 4 (Autumn 1994): 86.

83. Doug Clarke, "Defense Plant Sends Workers Home," Radio Free Europe/Radio Liberty *Daily Report*, September 1, 1994; Doug Clarke, "Another Defense Plant Furloughs Workers," Radio Free Europe/Radio Liberty *Daily Report*, December 2, 1994.

84. Wittneben, "Perspectives and the Role of U.S. Business in Russian Defense Conversion," p. 87.

85. Impuls produced components, including guidance systems, satellite systems, and electro-optics. It reduced its workforce from 3,000 employees in 1992 to 1,200 by the end of 1993. See Perlmutter, McFaul, and Naugle, "Impuls," pp. 48, 51.

CHAPTER 3

1. Because the problems of the Soviet government were dealt with in detail in the section on the Gorbachev period, the discussion here will focus on the era following the breakup of the Soviet Union.

2. For example, the decision to use the Russian military to crush Chechen resistance appears to have been made among a small number of members of the president's Security Council. Although the minister of defense participated in deliberations, critical institutions such as the general staff may not have. On the decision to intervene in Chechnya, see Robert Orttung, "More Details about the Decision to Intervene in Chechnya Come to Light," *OMRI Daily Digest*, Open Media Research Institute, Prague, February 7, 1995; and Robert Orttung, "More Revelations about Beginning of Chechen War," *OMRI Daily Digest*, Open Media Research Institute, Prague, February 8, 1995. For another discussion of contradictory initiatives from Moscow on cooperation with NATO and the development of Russian bases in the so-called near abroad, see Steven Erlanger, "Yeltsin's On-and-Off Decrees on Bases Cloud the Policy Outlook," *New York Times*, April 8, 1994, p. A5.

3. See Sergey Gorlenko, "Vmesto shifrogram—ankety: Zachem shpionam shpionit', kogda rossiyanye sami vsyo passkazhut" (Instead of a Coded Message—Questionaires: Why Should Spies Spy when Russians Themselves Will Tell All), *Rossiyskaya Gazeta* (Moscow), September 3, 1994, p. 3; and Sonni Efron, "Russia Livid over Alleged Spying by U.S.," *Los Angeles Times*, September 7, 1994, p. 1.

4. See Valeriy Fomichev, "Del'tsy ot oborony shturmuyut bastiony:

predpriyatiya strategicheskogo znacheniya stanovyatsya chastnoy sob-stvennost'yu" (Dealers from Defense Are Storming the Bastions; Enterprises of Strategic Importance Becoming Private Property), *Rossiyskaya Gazeta* (Moscow), January 17, 1995, p. 3.

5. See interview (by unidentified correspondent) with A. A. Kokoshin, first deputy minister of defense of the Russian Federation, on the "Aty Baty" program, Moscow Russian Television and Dubl Networks, 2305 GMT, April 17, 1993, translated in Foreign Broadcast Information Service—Soviet Union Affairs (hereafter, FBIS-SOV) 93-073, pp. 51–52; and A. A. Kokoshin, "Protivorechiya formirovaniya i puti razvitiya voenno-tekhnicheskoy politiki Rossiy" (Contradictions of Formation and Ways of Developing the Military-Technical Policy of Russia), *Voyennaya Mysl'* (Moscow), no. 2 (1993).

6. For example, in the tank industry the Ministry of Defense has reduced its support for producers from five to two enterprises. In the submarine and nuclear-powered shipbuilding industry all future procurement and repair orders will be concentrated with the Sevmash association in Severodvinsk. See Kokoshin, "Protivorechiya formirovaniya"; and Valentin Rudenko, "My sposobny proizvodit' unikal'noye oruzhiye i etu sposobnost' nel'zya uteryat'" (We Are Capable of Producing Unique Weapons and This Capability Must Not Be Lost), *Krasnaya Zvezda* (Moscow), March 11, 1993, p. 2.

7. In a March 1994 meeting of the Cabinet, Acting Finance Minister Sergey Dubinin reportedly charged that the defense industry had already placed procurement orders for 1994 worth 28 trillion rubles, while the budget allocation for this purpose was only 5 trillion rubles. See Keith Bush, "Budget Maneuvers Continue," Radio Free Europe/Radio Liberty *Daily Report*, March 4, 1994; and Keith Bush, "Defense Industry Wants More," Radio Free Europe/Radio Liberty *Daily Report*, March 30, 1994.

8. Chubays left the GKI to become first deputy prime minister in November 1994. He was initially replaced by a conservative, Vladimir Polevanov, who quickly got himself fired and was replaced by Belayev in February 1995.

9. The January 1994 state program on privatization specifically permits foreign ownership of shares in Russian defense enterprises, unless otherwise forbidden. See "Gosudarstvennaya programma privatizatsii gosudarstvennykh i munitsipal'nykh predpriyatiy v Rossiyskoy Federatsii" (State Program of Privatization of State and Municipal Enterprises in the Russian Federation), *Rossiyskiye Vesti* (Moscow), January 5, 1994, p. 3. Not surprisingly, defense industry advocates have since sought to limit the rights of foreigners in owning shares of defense enterprises. See Doug Clarke, "60 Percent of Defense Industry to Be Privatized," Radio Free Europe/Radio Liberty *Daily Report*, November 16, 1994.

10. See Vasiliy Ustyuzhanin, "The Situation in the VPK Is Threatening," *Federatsiya*, July 6, 1993, p. 2, translated in Joint Publications Research Service—

Soviet Union Military Affairs (hereafter, JPRS-UMA) 93-029, pp. 5–6; Andrey Simonov, "Hearings in the Supreme Soviet Defense Committee: Military Experts Propose Downsizing Defense Complex," *Kommersant-Daily* (Moscow), July 7, 1993, p. 4, translated in FBIS-SOV 93-128, pp. 32–33; and author interviews with defense enterprise directors, Moscow, April 1994.

11. See Chrystia Freeland, "Yeltsin 'Involved in Setting Up Oil Exporter,'" *Financial Times* (London), January 30, 1995, p. 3.

12. Like many Russian decrees, this order seems somewhat farfetched. Its implementation would require large numbers of enterprises engaged in foreign transactions to wait for clearance from probably uncooperative bureaucrats. None of the three bureaucracies, furthermore, has any history of carrying out these functions. See Government of the Russian Federation, resolution no. 1399 of December 19, 1994, *O merakh stabilizatsii ekonomicheskogo polozheniya predpriyatiy i organizatsiy oboronnogo kompleksa* (On Stabilization Measures of the Economic Situation of Enterprises and Organizations of the Defense Complex), *Ekonomika i zhizn'* (Moscow), no. 1 (January 1995): 7 supp.

13. See the comments of the Russian Labor Ministry spokesman in Penny Morvant, "Officials Say 40% of Income Hidden from Tax Inspectors," *OMRI Daily Digest*, Open Media Research Institute, Prague, April 20, 1995.

14. Rogov predicted that the government would collect only 70 trillion rubles, out of expected revenues of 124 trillion rubles in 1994. See Sergey Rogov, "Ustoyat li vooruzheninyye sily Rossiy? Zabytaya voyennaya reforma" (Will the Russian Armed Forces Hold Their Ground? The Forgotten Military Reform), *Nezavisimaya Gazeta* (Moscow), November 3, 1994, pp. 1, 5.

15. See Vitaliy Y. Vitebskiy, head of the main directorate of information and statistics of Goskomoboronprom, "VPK: Itogi 1994 goda" (The MIC: 1994 Results), mimeo, January 20, 1995.

16. Anders Åslund, *How Russia Became a Market Economy* (Washington, D.C.: Brookings Institution, 1995).

17. See, for example, the complaints from the director of NPO Impuls, which did not receive a government energy subsidy because its books were balanced. Tova Perlmutter, Michael McFaul, and Elaine Naugle, "Impuls," in David Bernstein, ed., *Defense Industry Restructuring in Russia: Case Studies and Analysis* (Stanford, Calif.: Center for International Security and Arms Control, December 1994), p. 47. The management of the Saratov Aviation Plant was similarly burned when the government intervened and offset enterprise debts in mid-1992. The Saratov plant reportedly was one of the few plants that had been keeping balanced books. See interview by Vitaliy Kovalenko with Vice Premier Valeriy Makhardze, "Reform Needs More People to Do Donkeywork," *Rossiyskaya Gazeta* (Moscow), September 4, 1992, p. 3, translated in FBIS-SOV 92-175, pp. 18–21.

18. Interview by V. Starkov with Chernomyrdin, "V. Chernomyrdin: 'I Will Not Be Distracted!'" *Argumenty i Fakty* (Moscow), no. 13 (March 1994): 1, 3, translated in FBIS-USR 94-034, pp. 1–5.

19. Author interviews, Perm' oblast and municipal government officials, April 1994 and May 1995.

20. See, for example, David Lipton and Jeffrey Sachs, "Privatization in Eastern Europe: The Case of Poland," *Brookings Papers on Economic Activity*, Brookings Institution, Washington, D.C., 1990, p. 294.

21. Note that privatization is not in itself a sufficient condition for the creation of hard-budget constraints if the state continues to subsidize the enterprise or if the management is confident that the state will not permit it to go bankrupt. See Janos Kornai, *The Road to a Free Economy—Shifting from a Socialist System: The Example of Hungary* (New York: W. W. Norton & Company, 1990), pp. 48–49.

22. After all, who needed unions in the workers' state? On Soviet-era trade unions, see Alec Nove, *The Soviet Economic System*, 2d ed. (London: Allen & Unwin, 1980), pp. 224–26; and Peter Rutland, "Labor Unrest and Movements in 1989 and 1990," *Soviet Economy* 6, no. 4 (October–December 1990): 347–49. Interestingly, the primary holdover union from the Soviet era, the Federation of Independent Trade Unions of Russia (FNPR), has sought to limit the influence of new, truly independent trade unions. See, for example, Viktor Khamrayev, "Svobodnyye profsoyuzy vystupayut protiv monopolixma nezavisimykh" (Free Trade Unions Speak Out against Independent Trade Unions' Monopolism), *Segodnya* (Moscow), May 4, 1995, p. 2. On the weakness of defense industry trade unions, see the comments of Anatoliy Breusov, chairman of the Association of Trade Unions of the Defense Industry, in "V 2005 godu lish' 5-7% vooruzheniy Rossiy budut otvechat' trebovaniyam vremeni" (In the Year 2005 Only 5–7 Percent of Russia's Arms Will Meet the Requirements of the Times), *Nezavisimaya Gazeta* (Moscow), November 24, 1994, pp. 4–5.

23. See Michael McFaul, "Agency Problems in the Privatization of Large Enterprises in Russia," in Michael McFaul and Tova Perlmutter, eds., *Privatization, Conversion, and Enterprise Reform in Russia* (Stanford, Calif.: Center for International Security and Arms Control, May 1994), p. 45.

24. As far back as 1991, Simon Johnson and Heidi Kroll detected that enterprise managers preferred to permit worker control of their enterprises, rather than allowing "strangers" to come in and control them. Johnson and Kroll found that none of the directors they interviewed feared that newly empowered workers would oust them. See Simon Johnson and Heidi Kroll, "Managerial Strategies for Spontaneous Privatization," *Soviet Economy* 7, no. 4 (October–December 1991): 308.

25. This is a peculiarity of the defense industry. In the civilian industries, these shares are sold off to the public. See Clifford G. Gaddy,

Civilianizing Russia: How Factories and Families are Adjusting to Life in a Non-militarized Economy (Washington, D.C.: Brookings Institution, forthcoming).

26. See Article 6, presidential ukase no. 1267 (classified), *Ob osobennostyakh privatizatsii i dopolnitel'nykh merakh gosudarstvennogo regulirovaniya deyatel'nosti predpriyatiy oboronykh otrasley promyshlennosti* (On the Special Features of Privatization and Supplementary Measures of State Regulation of the Activity of Enterprises of the Defense Sectors of Industry), August 19, 1993; and Russian Federation government decree no. 194 signed by Viktor Chernomyrdin, *Approval of Statute on Certification for the Right to Manage Enterprises and Organizations Developing and/or Producing Arms, Military Equipment and Ammunition and Their Main Components, Completing Articles and Materials*, reprinted in translation in JPRS-UMA 95-016, pp. 6–8.

27. See, for example, Alexander Kovalev and Sergei Chikker, "Defense, Engineering Plants Go for a Song," *Commersant* (Moscow), October 6, 1993, pp. 13–14.

28. Author interviews with an expert in a Russian Academy of Sciences institute, April 1994.

29. See, for example, Center for Economic Conditions under the Russian Federation Government, "Defense Enterprises and Their 1994 Prospects," a *Delovoy Mir* survey of 158 defense enterprises, August 27, 1994, p. 5.

30. Speech of Premier Viktor Chernomyrdin at the July 15, 1994, Russian Federation government session, "Sterzhen' raboty Pravitel'stva vo vtorom polugodii—strukturnaya perestroyka khozyaystva" (The Core of the Government's Work in the Second Half of the Year—Restucturing the Economy), *Rossiyskiye Vesti* (Moscow), July 19, 1994, pp. 1, 4; and Mikhail Berger, "Prem'yer predostereg Lenyu Golubkova i nesostoyatel'nyye predpriyatiya" (The Premier Warns Lenya Golubkov and Bankrupt Enterprises), *Izvestiya* (Moscow), July 16, 1994, p. ?

31. McFaul, "Agency Problems in the Privatization of Large Enterprises in Russia," p. 42. Alternatively, one could say that the managers possess the *economic* property rights over their enterprises. Yoram Barzel defines the economic property rights of individuals over assets as "the rights, or the powers, to consume, obtain income from, and alienate these assets." *Legal* rights, on the other hand, "enhance economic rights, but the former are neither necessary nor sufficient for the existence of the latter." See Yoram Barzel, *Economic Analysis of Property Rights* (New York: Cambridge University Press, 1989), p. 2. The author thanks Cliff Gaddy for highlighting this argument.

32. Author interview with a design bureau director, Washington, D.C., February 1994.

33. Author interview with the director of a joint-stock company, St. Petersburg, April 1994.

34. Author interview with Yevgeny Fedosev, director of GosNIIAS, Moscow, April 1994.

35. Johnson, Kroll, and Eder argue that there is necessarily some transfer of *residual control rights*—"the *de facto* ability to determine how a firm's assets are used in all circumstances other than those specified in implicit or explicit contracts." But the author found no basis for this observation in the numerous defense enterprises studied. See Simon Johnson, Heidi Kroll, and Santiago Eder, "Strategy, Structure, and Spontaneous Privatization in Russia and Ukraine," in Vedat Milor, ed., *Changing Political Economies: Privatization in Post-Communist and Reforming Communist States* (Boulder, Colo.: Lynne Rienner Publishers, 1993), pp. 147, 158; and author interviews with defense plant directors and management officials in Washington, D.C., February 1994, and in Moscow, Perm', and St. Petersburg, April 1994.

36. See, for example, Paul L. Joskow, Richard Schmalensee, and Natasha Tsukanova, "Competition Policy in Russia during and after Privatization," in *Microeconomics 1994* (Washington, D.C.: Brookings Institution, 1994), pp. 344–47.

37. Ibid., p. 347. Earlier, such cross-ownership appears to have been legal under the 1990 Law on Enterprises. See the discussion in Johnson and Kroll, "Managerial Strategies for Spontaneous Privatization," p. 289.

CHAPTER 4

1. See Joseph S. Berliner, *Soviet Industry from Stalin to Gorbachev: Essays on Management and Innovation* (Ithaca, N.Y.: Cornell University Press, 1988); Janos Kornai, "The Hungarian Reform Process: Visions, Hopes, and Reality," *Journal of Economic Literature* 24, no. 4 (December 1986); Ronald Amann and Julian Cooper, *Technical Progress and Soviet Economic Development* (Oxford: Basil Blackwell, 1986); and Gertrude Schroeder, *The System versus Progress: Soviet Economic Problems* (London: Centre for Research into Communist Economies, 1986).

2. See Gertrude Schroeder, *The System versus Progress*, pp. 42–43, 88.

3. See, for example, Vitali Naishul, "Institutional Development in the USSR," *Cato Journal* 11, no. 3 (Winter 1992): 490, 492; and Thane Gustafson, *Crisis amid Plenty: The Politics of Soviet Energy under Brezhnev and Gorbachev* (Princeton, N.J.: Princeton University Press, 1989), p. 309.

4. This was true for civilian enterprises, as well. See, for example, Jan Winiecki, "Large Industrial Enterprises in Soviet-type Economies: The Ruling Stratum's Main Rent-Seeking Area," *Communist Economies* 1, no. 4 (1989): 363–83.

5. Another way to describe rent, here in contrast to the traditional consumer's conception of the term, is as "allocatively unnecessary payment not required to attract resources to a particular employment." See James M. Buchanan, "Rent Seeking and Profit Seeking," in James M. Buchanan

and Gordon Tullock, eds., *Toward a Theory of the Rent-Seeking Society* (College Station, Tex.: Texas A&M University, 1980), pp. 3–7.

6. For example, a firm's resources can also be directed to production, distribution, etc. See Anne O. Krueger, "The Political Economy of the Rent-Seeking Society," *American Economic Review* 64, no. 3 (June 1974): 293.

7. Yevgeniy Kuznetsov, "Adjustment of the Russian Defence-Related Enterprises: Macroeconomic Implications," mimeo, Institute for Economic Forecasting, Moscow, October 1993, p. 16.

8. See Ferenc Feher et al., *Dictatorship over Needs: An Analysis of Soviet Societies* (New York: St. Martin's Press, 1983), p. 248.

9. See Oleg Antonov, "VPK Mertv: O maloizvestnykh prichinakh krizisa na predpriyatiyakh voeyenno-promyshlennogo kompleksa" (The MIC Is Dead: About Little-Known Reasons for the Crisis at Enterprises of the Military-Industrial Complex), *Nezavisimaya Gazeta* (Moscow), September 1, 1994, p. 4.

10. On paternalism, see Clifford G. Gaddy, "Notes for a Theory of the Paternalistic Russian Enterprise," mimeo, November 18, 1994; and the case of MCST in David Bernstein and Elaine Naugle, "ELVIS+ and the Moscow Center for SPARC Technology (MCST)," in David Bernstein, ed., *Defense Industry Restructuring in Russia: Case Studies and Analysis* (Stanford, Calif.: Center for International Security and Arms Control, December 1994), p. 39.

11. Kokoshin writes: "Analysis of a whole range of actual situations in which decisions were taken on the development of armaments shows that, in defense technology and in industry as a whole, *party and state organs of the USSR gave preference to impressive systems that looked good on their reports*" (author's emphasis). See Andrey Kokoshin, "Defense Industry Conversion in the Russian Federation," in Teresa Pelton Johnson and Steven E. Miller, eds., *Russian Security after the Cold War: Seven Views from Moscow* (McLean, Va.: Brassey's, 1994), footnote 3; and Vladimir Aleksandrovich Ponomarenko, untitled article in *Vooruzheniye, Politika, Konversiya* 4, no. 1 (August 4, 1994): 17–20, translated in Joint Publications Research Service—Soviet Union Military Affairs (hereafter, JPRS-UMA) 94-056, pp. 12–14.

12. See Peter Almquist, "Soviet Military Acquisition: From a Seller's Market to a Buyer's?" in Susan L. Clark, ed., *Soviet Military Power in a Changing World* (Boulder, Colo.: Westview Press, 1991); Matthew Partan, "Who Controlled the Former-Soviet Military Industry?" *Soviet Defense Notes* (MIT Post-Soviet Security Studies Working Group) 4, no. 1 (March 1992); and author interviews with a Soviet General Staff official, Cambridge, Mass., September 1992, and with defense enterprise directors, Moscow, April 1994.

13. For a characteristic expression of this argument, see S. Gubanov, "Mekhanism konversii: problemy i perspektivy (po materialam konferentsii Ligi sodeystviya oboronnym predpriyatiyam)" (A Mechanism of

Conversion: Problems and Perspectives [from the materials of a Conference of the League of Assistance to Defense Enterprises]), *Ekonomist* (Moscow), no. 7 (July 1993): 50–61.

14. Author interview with a design bureau director, Moscow region, April 1994.

15. See Oleg Rosnitkiy, "'Oborona i oboronka': Vremya soglsovyvat' interesy'" (Defense and the Defense Industry: It's Time to Reconcile Interests), *Nezavisimaya Gazeta* (Moscow), August 14, 1992, p. 2. See also the similar complaints of Western investors who have attempted to start joint ventures with Russian partners, as summarized in Aleksei K. Ponomarev, "Prospects for Russian-American Business Cooperation in Defense Conversion," in Michael P. Claudon and Kathryn Wittneben, eds. *After the Cold War: Russian-American Defense Conversion for Economic Renewal* (New York: New York University Press, 1993), pp. 20–21.

16. Antonov, "VPK Mertv."

17. Author interviews with defense enterprise managers in Moscow, Perm', and St. Petersburg, April 1994; and Andrei Kuznetsov, "Economic Reforms in Russia: Enterprise Behaviour as an Impediment to Change," *Europe-Asia Studies* (Glasgow) 46, no. 6 (1994): 967.

18. Adi Ignatius, "U.S. Stirs Russian Resentment with Plans for Defense Conversion," *Wall Street Journal*, September 19, 1994, p. 10.

19. See Schroeder, *System versus Progress*, pp. 42–43.

20. See Kuznetsov, "Economic Reforms in Russia," pp. 963–64.

21. See the survey results of Y. N. Kulichkov and V. D. Kalachapov, "Analysis of Production-Economic Activities of Enterprises of the Defense Branches of Industry under the Conditions of the Conversion of Military Production," *Voprosy Ekonomiki i Konversii*, no. 1 (1994): 3–8, translated in JPRS-UMA 94-038, pp. 22–25.

22. Author interviews with city and oblast officials, Perm', April 1994; Clifford G. Gaddy, "Russian Wage Tax Legislation and 'Dead Souls,'" mimeo, March 4, 1994; and A. Z. Belyalov, *Rekomendatsii—Kak izbezhat' bol'shikh rossiyskikh nalogov: Prakticheskoye rukovodstvo* (Recommendations—How to Avoid Large Russian Taxes: A Practical Guide) (Moscow: Aytolan, 1992).

23. Author site visits to defense plants, Moscow region, Perm', and St. Petersburg, April–May 1994.

24. See Yuriy Lepskiy, "Armor," *Trud* (Moscow), September 19, 1992, p. 5 translated in JPRS-UMA 92-040, pp. 45–48. This phenomenon appears to be widespread in the aviation sector as well. The MiG-producing Moscow Aviation Production Association has continued to turn out MiG-29s using its own resources after the state orders stopped coming in. See Vladimir Kuzmin, "Ne upustit' MiG" (Don't Give Up MiG), *Rossiyskiye Vesti* (Moscow), August 6, 1992, p. 3.

25. Julian Cooper, "The Soviet Defence Industry Heritage and Economic Restructuring in Russia," in Lars B. Wallin, ed., *The Post-Soviet Military-Industrial*

Complex (Stockholm: Swedish Nations Defence Research Establishment, 1994), p. 37, drawing on the FOA Symposium, Stockholm, October 20, 1993; and V. Golovachev, "The Collapse of the Defense Complex May Cause the Crash of the Economy," *Ekonomika i Zhizn'* (Moscow), no. 18 (May 1992).

26. Vitaliy Shlykov, "The Defense Industry and Democracy in Russia: The Interplay," mimeo, Fall 1993.

27. Ibid.

28. For an excellent analysis of this phenomenon, see Barry W. Ickes and Randi Ryterman, "Roadblock to Economic Reform: Inter-Enterprise Debt and the Transition to Markets," *Post-Soviet Affairs* 9, no. 3 (July–September 1993): 231–52.

29. Ibid.

30. Shlykov, "Defense Industry and Democracy in Russia."

31. The central Bank provided commercial banks with credits for loans to debtor enterprises. However, the interest rates on these credits were concessionary—considerably less than the inflation rate. Because the Central Bank was responsible to the Russian Supreme Soviet, which had little interest in macroeconomic stabilization, it was able to act independently of the government's wishes.

32. Ickes and Ryterman, "Roadblock to Economic Reform," p. 240.

33. S. Tsekhmistrenko, "Monopolist mostit dorogu na rynok blagimi namereniyami" (Monopolist Paves the Road to the Market with Good Intentions), *Kommersant-Daily* (Moscow), March 24, 1994, p. 4.

34. See Doug Clarke, "Kokoshin Says State Must Pay Defense Debts," *OMRI Daily Digest,* Open Media Research Institute, Prague, February 9, 1995; and Sergey Rogov, "Ustoyat li vooruzheninyye sily Rossiy? Zabytaya voyennaya reforma" (Will the Russian Armed Forces Hold Their Ground? The Forgotten Military Reform), *Nezavisimaya Gazeta* (Moscow), November 3, 1994, pp. 1, 5.

35. Author interviews and site visit at NPO Mashinostroyeniya, Moscow region, April 1994.

36. See memorandum from A. N. Ilyushenko in "Transfer of Federal Property into Hands of Private Business Occurring at Defense Industry Enterprises," *Rabochaya Tribuna* (Moscow), January 25, 1995, pp. 1–2, translated in Foreign Broadcast Information Service—Soviet Union Affairs (hereafter, FBIS-SOV) 95-019, pp. 40–42.

37. Yevgeniy Kuznetsov, personal communication with the author.

38. Author interview with design bureau director, Wye Plantation, Md., February 1994.

39. Author interviews with a city official, Perm', April 1994 and May 1995, and personal communication with Yevgeniy Kuznetsov.

40. Tarja Cronberg, "Enterprise Strategies to Cope with Reduced Defense Spending: The Experience of the Perm Region," in Michael McFaul and Tova

Perlmutter, eds., *Privatization, Conversion, and Enterprise Reform in Russia* (Stanford, Calif.: Center for International Security and Arms Control, May 1994), pp. 193–94.

41. Author interview with a conversion department director of a defense enterprise, Moscow region, April 1994.

42. Author interviews with defense enterprise directors, Moscow region and St. Petersburg, April 1994.

43. McFaul, "Agency Problems in the Privatization of Large Enterprises in Russia," in McFaul and Perlmutter, *Privatization, Conversion, and Enterprise Reform*, p. 43.

44. "The Jane's Interview" (unattributed) with Andrey Kokoshin, Russian Federation first deputy minister of defense, *Jane's Defence Weekly* (London), June 25, 1994, p. 32.

45. Speech of Premier Viktor Chernomyrdin at the July 15, 1994, Russian Federation government session, "Sterzhen' raboty Pravitel'stva vo vtorom polugodii—strukturnaya perestroyka khozyaystva" (The Core of the Government's Work in the Second Half of the Year—Restructuring the Economy), *Rossiyskiye Vesti* (Moscow), July 19, 1994, pp. 1, 4.

46. On spin-offs generally, see David Bernstein, "Spin-offs and Start-ups in Russia: A Key Element of Industrial Restructuring," in McFaul and Perlmutter, *Privatization, Conversion, and Enterprise Reform*, pp. 201–15.

47. Author interviews with defense enterprise directors and staffs, Moscow region, Perm', and St. Petersburg, April 1994.

48. Ibid.; and the example of MCST in Bernstein and Naugle, "ELVIS+ and the Moscow Center for SPARC Technology," p. 41.

49. Author interview with the director and staff of a joint-stock company, St. Petersburg, April 1994.

50. Otto Latsis, "Conversion Troubles: The Hardest Thing to Do Is What You Do Not Wish to Do," *Izvestiya* (Moscow), July 4, 1992, p. 3, translated in JPRS-UMA 92-028, pp. 38–40.

51. Kuznetsov, "Economic Reforms in Russia," p. 967; and author interviews with Russian defense enterprise managers, Wye Plantation, Md., and Washington, D.C., February 1994, and Moscow region, Perm', and St. Petersburg, April 1994.

52. Clifford Gaddy, *Civilizing Russia: How Factories and Families Are Adjusting to Life in a Non-militarized Economy* (Washington, D.C.: Brookings Institution, forthcoming).

53. Author interview with an institute director, Perm', April 1994.

54. On the League of Defense Enterprises, see Pavel Fel'gengauer, "Vsye v Rossii khotyat torgovat' oruzhiyem" (Everyone in Russia Wants to Trade in Weapons), *Nezavisimaya Gazeta* (Moscow), October 1, 1992, p. 2.

55. See the comments of Yevgeniy Lenskiy, adviser to the first deputy prime minister Oleg Soskovets, in Aleksandr Golyayev, "Konkurenty

beskhozyaystvennosti" (Competitors of Mismanagement), *Rossiyskaya Gazeta* (Moscow), March 17, 1994, p. 3.

56. On defense manager views of FPGs, see Gubanov, "Mekhanism konversii."

57. See Roman Zadunayskiy, "Prezidentskiy Ukaz podderzhit oboronnyy zakaz" (A Presidential Edict Will Support the Defense Order), *Rossiyskiye Vesti* (Moscow), November 24, 1993, pp. 1–2. Adam Stulberg reports that Kokoshin also has cited as models the Biysk Chemical Combine, the Antey Production Association, NPO Almaz, the Mil helicopter design bureau, and the Khrunichev design bureau. See Adam N. Stulberg, "The High Politics of Arming Russia," *RFE/RL Research Report 2*, no. 49 (December 10, 1993): 5.

58. In a revealing example, a reporter investigating the formation of the Russian Aerospace Company (RAK) found that no one in any of the enterprises reported to be part of the FPG had ever heard of it. See Mikhail Chernyshev, "Trest, kotoryy . . . Idei Manilova priobreli kosmicheskiy masshtab" (The Trust Which . . . Manilov's Ideas Acquire Cosmic Scale), *Segodnya* (Moscow), September 15, 1994, p. 9.

59. Author interviews with Russian Academy of Sciences experts, Moscow, April–May 1994.

60. This section is based in part on Kevin P. O'Prey, *The Arms Export Challenge: Cooperative Export Management and Defense Conversion* (Washington, D.C.: Brookings Institution, 1995).

61. Economist Clifford Gaddy argues that throughout the 1980s, the Soviet government actually received less than $3 billion annually in hard currency. This reflects an assumption that only 25 percent of Soviet export transactions were for cash, and only 50–60 percent of the credit was repaid. See Gaddy, *Civilianizing Russia*.

For a Russian estimate of cash transactions amounting to one-third of all arms deliveries between 1986 and 1990, see Pavel Fel'gengauer, "Rezkoye sokrashcheniye eksporta otechestvennogo: oruzhiya vpervyye obyavleny ofitsial'nyye tsifry voyenno tekhnicheskogo sotrudnichestva za 1991 god" (Sharp Reduction in Exports of Our Weapons: The First Releases of Official Figures of Military-Technical Cooperation for 1991), *Nezavisimaya Gazeta* (Moscow), September 29, 1992, pp. 1–2.

62. See Pavel Fel'gengauer, "Torgovlya oruzhiyem ne tak vygodnaya Rossiy, kak utverzhdayet Rosvooruzheniye" (The Arms Trade Is Not as Beneficial to Russia as Rosvooruzheniye Asserts), *Segodnya* (Moscow), March 10, 1995, p. 2.

63. For example, in the deal that is sending MiG-29 combat aircraft to Malaysia, Moscow will accept one-quarter of the payment in the form of palm oil. Export agreements with India similarly allow for payment to Moscow in the form of tea as well as rupees. See Sergey Mashtakov, "MiG i v Malayzii: Kto eshche kupit nashi istrebiteli?" (MiG Also in Malaysia: Who Else Will Buy

Our Fighters?" *Rossiyskaya Gazeta* (Moscow), September 7, 1994, p. 3; and "Shibayev, Deputy Chairman of the Committee for Foreign Economic Relations: If Everyone Were Allowed to Sell Arms, the Unjustified Competition Would Lead to a Fall in Prices," *Komsomolskaya Pravda* (Moscow), February 25, 1992, p. 1, translated in FBIS-SOV 92-039, pp. 31–32.

64. The Russian government has attempted to use excess—or even newly procured—weapons to pay off its foreign debts. For example, it settled some of its debts to Hungary with exports of MiG-29 aircraft. See the discussion in Tsekhmistrenko, "Monopolist mostit dorogu na rynok blagimi namereniyami."

65. In a well-publicized case, in early 1995 the director/owner of a Yekaterinburg spin-off, Spetstekhnika, laid off two-thirds of his workforce (all of whom had been working on defense production) in order to focus on civilian work with the remaining one-third. The director planned to sell off all of his unused facilities. See U.S. Department of State cable, from the U.S. Embassy, Moscow, March 16, 1995, 1429 GMT.

66. Author interview with a city official, Perm', April 1994.

67. None of these phenomena apply to enterprises located in Moscow. Evidently, the arrangement for social obligations for Moscow enterprises was different than for enterprises in the rest of the country. It appears that most Moscow enterprises simply transferred resources to the city budget and were compensated by the city government's providing their workers with commensurate social services. Author interviews with defense enterprise officials, Moscow, April 1994.

68. Kuznetsov describes this group as the logical constituency for Yegor Gaydar's radical reform party, Russia's Choice. See Yevgeniy Kuznetsov, "Enterprise Adjustment and Interest Groups within the MIC," in Wallin, *Post-Soviet Military-Industrial Complex*, pp. 69–70.

CHAPTER 5

1. This concept was provided by a U.S. defense industry executive during an off-the-record discussion at a February 1994 Brookings Institution conference on arms exports. An expanded definition of the concept can be found in Kevin P. O'Prey, *The Arms Export Challenge: Cooperative Export Management and Defense Conversion* (Washington, D.C.: Brookings Institution, 1995).

2. Aspects of the argument presented here are shared by the January 1994 proposals from the U.S.-based Fund for Democracy and Development. See *A New Strategy for United States Assistance to Russia and the Newly Independent States: A Report of the Fund's Policy Panel*, Fund for Democracy and Development, Washington, D.C., January 10, 1994.

3. According to one report, imports have carved out a 40 percent share of the Russian consumer goods market. See Euan Craik, "Study: Imports

Capture 40% of Market," *Moscow Times*, November 27, 1994, pp. 47–48.

4. See David Bernstein, "Organizational Restructuring," in David Bernstein, ed., *Defense Industry Restructuring in Russia: Case Studies and Analysis* (Stanford, Calif.: Center for International Security and Arms Control, December 1994), p. 141; and Clifford Gaddy, personal communication to author, March 1995.

5. For an example of the growing paranoia that all Western business interest in the defense sector is really espionage, see Mikhail Rebrov, "Tramplin ili Lovushka? Zapadnyye razvedki menyayut metody, no ne tseli" (Springboard or Trap? Western Intelligence Agents Are Changing Their Methods, But Not Their Goals), *Krasnaya Zvezda* (Moscow), January 26, 1995, p. 3.

6. All U.S. aid to the former Soviet states during fiscal year 1994 amounted to $2.45 billion. However, funding has dropped off dramatically to a planned $850 million for all of the former Soviet Union (and $379 million for Russia) in fiscal year 1995. Fred Hiatt and Daniel Southerland, "Grass-Roots Aid Works Best in Russia," *Washington Post*, February 12, 1995, pp. A1, 36.

7. OPIC's direct loans typically range from $2 million to $10 million.

8. OPIC's loan guarantees are issued to U.S. lending institutions on behalf of eligible investors and typically range from $10 million to $200 million. See "Overseas Private Investment Corporation (OPIC)," Flashfax service, U.S. Department of Commerce, February 11, 1994.

9. See Overseas Private Investment Corporation, "NIS Defense Conversion," mimeo, Washington, D.C., 1995.

10. U.S. Russia Investment Fund press releases, New York, May 1995.

11. The four states that found themselves with a nuclear capability when the Soviet Union collapsed are Belarus, Kazakhstan, Russia, and Ukraine. All except for Russia have pledged to become nonnuclear states.

12. The Nunn-Lugar-supported International Science and Technology Center (ISTC) in Moscow and the Center for Science and Technology in Ukraine (STCU) have so far funded ninety-four projects worth $48.5 million and involving more than five thousand scientists and engineers. Author interview with a U.S. government official, March 1995.

13. See Theodor Galdi, "The Nunn-Lugar Cooperative Threat Reduction Program for Soviet Weapons Dismantlement: Background and Implementation," CRS Report to Congress 93-1057F, Congressional Research Service, December 29, 1993.

14. Flashfax service, U.S. Department of Commerce, June 13, 1994.

15. See "SecDef Announces Defense Conversion Contract Awards," news release, Office of the Assistant U.S. Secretary of Defense (Public Affairs), June 23, 1994.

16. Ibid.

17. Jeffrey M. Lenorovitz, "U.S.-Russian Teams Get Pentagon Funds," *Aviation Week and Space Technology*, August 8, 1994, p. 27.

18. Ibid.

19. For these enterprises, the connection to weapons of mass destruction is fairly broadly conceived. Each enterprise evidently need only be involved in some aspect of research, development, or production of weapons of mass destruction or their delivery systems. Thus, loosely related avionics design facilities could qualify under such criteria.

20. The five enterprises are NPO Kompozit, NPO Mashinostroyeniya, NPO Soyuz, Tupolev, and Energomash. See "Funds for Russian Defense Conversion," Flashfax service, U.S. Department of Commerce, February 2, 1994; and Tom McCabe, Defense Nuclear Agency contracting officer, remarks to Site-Visit Conference, Defense Nuclear Agency, Moscow, April 12, 1994.

21. Author interview with a U.S. government official, October 1994.

22. See "DOD Announces Defense Enterprise Fund Grant," news release, Office of the Assistant U.S. Secretary of Defense (Public Affairs), June 23, 1994.

23. Interview with a U.S. government official, July 1995.

24. See U.S. Department of State telegram, "US Firms Find Opportunities in the Defense Industry Sector," U.S. Consulate, St. Petersburg, February 7, 1995.

25. The DEF is also investing in a project in Belarus and another in Kazakhstan. See Defense Enterprise Fund, "Investments Approved by the Defense Enterprise Fund," press release, Boston, July 12, 1995.

26. Reportedly, the budget for these projects is relatively small—$12 million. Author interviews with a U.S. government official, July 1995.

27. Author interview with a U.S. government official, February 1995.

28. Ibid.

29. Japan has an 8.5 percent share, and the countries of the European Community and its institutions own a combined total of 53.7 percent. See "The European Bank for Reconstruction and Development," Flashfax service, U.S. Department of Commerce, February 11, 1994.

30. U.S. Department of State, "US Firms Find Opportunities in the Defense Industry Sector."

31. Author interview with a U.S. government official, February 1995.

32. The issue of U.S. aid monies going to high-priced "consultants" provokes outrage from critics in the United States and Russia alike. See, for example, Hiatt and Southerland, "Grass-Roots Aid Works Best in Russia"; and Fred Hiatt, "U.S. Firms Cash In on Projects," Washington Post, February 12, 1995, p. A36.

33. Interview with a U.S. government official, January 1995. The contracts-signed figure is in budget terms what the Department of Defense refers to as "obligations."

34. Fred Hiatt, "Paying Russia to Destroy Nuclear Weapons: Critics Call Program a Dud," Washington Post, February 12, 1995, p. A36.

35. Galdi, "Nunn-Lugar Cooperative Threat Reduction Program," p. 9.

36. This view is shared by Sergei Kortunov, the head of the Department of Export Control and Conversion, Russian Ministry of Foreign Affairs, who argues, "Cooperative ventures would provide access to Western economic, intellectual, and technological resources while commercializing advanced technologies developed by defense industries." See Sergei Kortunov, "Defense Conversion in Russia: The Need for Multilateral Support," in Michael P. Claudon and Kathryn Wittneben, eds., *After the Cold War: Russian-American Defense Conversion for Economic Renewal* (New York: New York University Press, 1993), p. 59.

37. Excellent examples of such activities can be found in Sun Microsystems' work with ELVIS+ and the partnership of the U.S. firm Astronautics and St. Petersburg's NII Elektropribor. See David Bernstein and Elaine Naugle, "ELVIS+ and the Moscow Center for SPARC Technology (MCST)," in David Bernstein, ed., *Defense Industry Restructuring in Russia: Case Studies and Analysis* (Stanford, Calif.: Center for International Security and Arms Control, December 1994), p. 30; and U.S. Department of State, "US Firms Find Opportunities in the Defense Industry Sector," p. 6.

38. See Kathryn Wittneben, "Perspectives and the Role of U.S. Business in Russian Defense Conversion," in Claudon and Wittneben, *After the Cold War*, p. 83.

39. About half of the U.S. companies are in the Fortune 500. Others are small, high-tech firms, start-ups, or consulting outfits. By industry, approximately 20 percent of the firms are involved in aerospace or avionics, 20 percent are in computers or telecommunications, and roughly 10 percent are smaller, high-tech or R&D firms. See "U.S./Russian Defense Conversion JVs Number from 70 to 80," *Russia Desk* (newsletter), Commerce Publishing International, Arlington, Va., January 2, 1995, p. 7.

40. A National Academy of Sciences proposal for similar conversion partnerships offers an even more innovative scheme for an investment fund. Under this proposal—a Russian-American Partnership for Industrial Development (RAPID)—the investment fund would be set up by the U.S. and Russian governments but would ultimately rely on selling shares to private investors as a means to raise capital. The initial government-financed investments would provide a portfolio with which to approach capital markets. In order to instill investor confidence, the governments would provide a joint guaranty for the full dollar amount of the original investments after five years from issuance. If the project were to fail, the costs of fulfilling the guaranty would not have a significant impact on the budgets of the U.S. and Russian governments until six or seven years from the program's inception, and the cash costs would be spread out over several years due to the issuance of the shares in vintage series.

If the Fund were to fail and the Russian government lacked adequate currency to cover its obligations, it could resort to transferring to the U.S. government ownership of extracted natural resources, or making offsets against U.S. government payments committed to Russia (such as funds to be transferred in exchange for Russian uranium). See Committee on Enterprise Management in a Market Economy under Defense Conversion, *A Russian Partnership for Industrial Development* (Washington, D.C.: National Academy Press, 1993), pp. 5–6.

41. Ibid., p. 5.

INDEX

ABOUT THE AUTHOR

K evin P. O'Prey is a member of the MIT Project on Post-Soviet Security, where he is completing a doctoral dissertation on change in the Soviet/Russian defense industries. Currently an associate at DFI International, a Washington, D.C., research and analysis firm, Mr. O'Prey is the author of *The Arms Export Challenge: Cooperative Approaches to Export Management and Defense Conversion* (Brookings Institution, 1995); *Regaining the High Ground: NATO's Stake in the New Talks on Conventional Armed Forces in Europe* (St. Martin's, 1990), with Barry M. Blechman and William J. Durch; and "Keeping the Peace in Borderlands of Russia," in William J. Durch, ed., *UN Peacekeeping, American Policy, and the Uncivil Wars of the 1990s* (Henry L. Stimson Center, forthcoming). Mr. O'Prey has conducted extensive research and interviews in Russia. His prior experience in Washington, D.C., includes the Brookings Institution, the Institute for Defense Analyses, and the Carnegie Endowment for International Peace.

RUSSIA IN TRANSITION

A SERIES OF TWENTIETH CENTURY FUND REPORTS examining the key issues post-Soviet Russia faces as it makes the change from communism to a market economy and struggles to find its place in the world.

ALSO AVAILABLE IN THIS SERIES:

ECOLOGICAL DISASTER

CLEANING UP THE HIDDEN LEGACY OF THE SOVIET REGIME

A TWENTIETH CENTURY FUND REPORT BY MURRAY FESHBACH

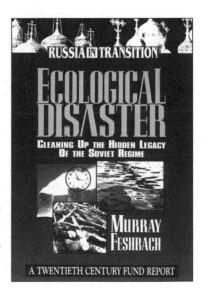

Feshbach makes the case for massive Western assistance stretching over decades to help undo the ecological destruction and reverse the conditions that lead to declining health that plague every part of the former Soviet Union.

Feshbach, a Georgetown University professor and noted Sovietologist, says "the breadth and depth of the health and environmental problems of the former Soviet Union have been understated."

He proposes a three-pronged approach to prevent future Chernobyls, attack the health crisis at the human level, and build health and ecological alliances among the Russian people. "For the West to ignore this problem would be an act of considerable indifference and callousness in the face of a clear humanitarian crisis."

ISBN: 0-87078-364-5, paper, 157 pages, $9.95

To order *Ecological Disaster*, call 1-800-275-1447 Washington, D.C. residents call 797-6258

Visit the Twentieth Century Fund's World Wide Web Site at http://epn.org./tcf.html

DEFENSE CONVERSION
TRANSFORMING THE ARSENAL OF DEMOCRACY
A Twentieth Century Fund Book, By Jacques S. Gansler

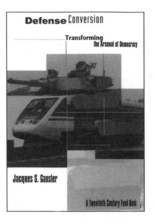

DEFENSE CONVERSION offers solid proposals for making the U.S. defense sector a thriving, integrated civilian/military operation that maintains the nation's military strength in a time of reduced defense budgets—without sacrificing technological superiority or a strong industrial base. Gansler, former Deputy Assistant Secretary of Defense, says the government must play a major role if this conversion is to succeed.

Anyone who is interested in national security, America's competitiveness, or jobs will be both informed and challenged by Gansler's fascinating book on defense conversion.

256 pages; 0–262–07166–5; $25.00; Cloth
Published by The MIT Press

To order DEFENSE CONVERSION, call
1-800-356-0343.